Sew Cute and Collectible

SOCK
Monkeys

Sew Cute and Collectible

SOCK
Monkeys

For Red-Heel Sock Monkey Crafters and Collectors

DEE LINDNER,
THE SOCK MONKEY LADY®

Creative Publishing
international

Creative Publishing international

First published in the United States of America by
Creative Publishing international, a division of
Quarto Publishing Group USA Inc.
400 First Avenue North
Suite 400
Minneapolis, MN 55401
1-800-328-3895
www.creativepub.com
Visit www.Craftside.net for a behind-the-scenes peek at our crafty world!

Visit www.sockmonkeylady.com
For *Socksillyumptuous* Monkey Muse
and Whimsical Gifts

ISBN: 978-1-58923-866-4

Digital edition published in 2015
eISBN: 978-1-62788-272-9
10 9 8 7 6 5 4 3 2 1

Library of Congress Cataloging-in-Publication Data
available

Copy Editor: Karen Levy
Proofreader: Breanne Subias
Cover Design and Layout: Laura Mcfadden Design, Inc.
Illustrations: Gayle Isabelle Ford
Photographs: Dee Lindner

Printed in China

"Science does not know its debt to imagination."
—Ralph Waldo Emerson

 To Gary and Peetie

DEDICATION

A special thanks to all who have turned to our endearing red-heel
sock monkeys for comfort and companionship. Together, we are many,
we are of a kindred spirit, and we believe in make-believe.

Contents

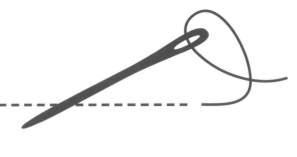

Introduction

Red-heel sock monkeys share our dreams, witness our mischievous antics, and listen to our inner desires. They feel the tug of little and big hands in moments of desperation and exhilaration. Stained with tears of sorrow and laughter, they behold heartfelt stories from one generation to the next. Most of all, they reflect the resilient human spirit.

Dee Lindner, the Sock Monkey Lady®, known internationally for her adorable red-heel sock monkey creations and endearing sock monkey action photography, invites you to enter the world of sock monkeys. Join her and be immersed in a place where sock monkey shenanigans and sock monkey vernacular abound—a place where monkey magic and make-believe begin—a place where *socksillyumptuous* red-heel sock monkeys reign and do what they do best: make us smile with their lovable humor.

The art of make-believe is something children do naturally, and something adults often lose as the world becomes familiar and predictable. For generations, sock monkeys have served as our guide to open secret places where make-believe hides, awaiting those who take life less seriously and who believe in the magic of sock monkeys.

Sew Cute and Collectible Sock Monkeys is stuffed with insight into the red-heel sock monkey tradition and ideas of how you can "monkey around" and make your own magical monkey moments. The Sock Monkey Lady® shares her tips, quips, and techniques on how to create and dress your own ideal, one-of-kind, handmade collectible sock monkey for all generations to enjoy. Her expertise is offered as a platform on which to craft or build a collection of endearing red-heel sock monkeys. Fun ideas of how to bring your sock monkey to life come together amid her engaging action-oriented photographs of sock monkeys from her collection to give you inspiration to rock, sock, cut, and sew!

Sock monkey mania has stirred the world! Whether you are a sock monkey crafter, collector, or caregiver, let the sock monkey fever fill your *sole*. The art of crafting unique, handmade, red-heel sock monkeys has taken twists and turns, with today's crafters giving sock monkeys of yesteryear a new look in the twenty-first century, making them more desirable than ever. Cute, collectible, charming, funny, and funky—yesterday's and today's new wave of sock monkey creations will have you in stitches whether you are sewing or looking for an ideal sock mate to collect or gift!

SECTION

I

Sock Monkey
Mania

Universal Appeal

Sock monkey enthusiasts love to talk about sock monkeys! Many people know about the red-heel sock monkey tradition and either have a comical and endearing sock monkey in their lives or know of someone who does. Others even make it their business to monkey around on their own or through organizations!

Sock monkey interest around the world is skyrocketing! Search engine hits for "sock monkey" have increased nearly 7,000 percent over the last decade. While these climbing cyberspace statistics are caused by a number of factors in the marketplace, few can refute sock monkey fever is spreading around the world and is taking a toehold. The advent of the Internet, e-mail, cell phones, and other connectivity mechanisms lets us easily share our sock monkey enthusiasm with the click of a button. And in our mobile society, monkeys are on the move as they accompany us to new job or retirement locations, or to vacation destinations at home and abroad.

Today's culture of ingenuity allows sock monkey enthusiasts to delight in an explosion of sock monkey novelty items, seemingly sprung overnight—all stemming from a folk art tradition steeped in character and silly shenanigans. A plethora of sock monkey items are internationally available through major retail chains, gift shops, and online businesses. Never before has the joy of monkeying around been easier!

To most sock monkey enthusiasts, this craze of monkeying around is not about money—it's about intrinsic value: the art of monkey-making if you are a crafter, the thrill of the hunt if you are a collector, and the grins and giggles if you are a caregiver, relishing priceless smiles and laughter with family, friends, and loved ones. Plain and simple, it's about the monkey.

Sock monkey fever continues to spread through their appearances in day-to-day life or in commercials, television shows, and movies. They garner interest and steal hearts as they take their rightful place as pop culture icons.

Affordable Creations

If you have not had the good fortune of being gifted a one-of-a-kind, handmade red-heel sock monkey—and doubt you ever will—there are *sockonomic* ways to monkey around!

Red-heel socks knitted and trademarked by the Nelson Knitting Company (NKC) of Rockford, Illinois, from which red-heel sock monkeys were originally crafted are commonly referred to as vintage. Even though NKC is no longer in business, their socks can still be found in the marketplace. These hard-to-find socks, considered rare, can be pricey, as their availability is limited.

Fox River Mills, Inc. (FRM), which acquired NKC, continues to manufacture the red-heel socks with slight changes. These red-heel socks, referred to herein as modern, can be found on the Internet in units of one pair per pack, two pairs per pack, or bundles of differing quantities.

Periodically, red-heel socks with slight flaws are sold as "seconds" at reduced prices—a boon to crafters deft with a needle who enjoy further savings.

If your lifestyle is too busy for you to create a sock monkey, buy a ready-to-love handmade monkey created from either style of red-heel socks, or commission a crafter

There are a number of other companies that knit socks from which sock monkeys are commercially manufactured or uniquely handmade. Only the monkeys sewn from red-heel socks manufactured by NKC and subsequently by FRM are primarily included in this work, for they provide the foundation of the red-heel sock monkey tradition.

to make one for you. Prices vary widely depending on the skill level of the maker and the monkey's details and personalization.

There are a number of different outlets where you can purchase vintage or modern red-heel socks and new or already-loved handmade red-heel monkeys. They can be purchased at website stores, online auctions, bazaars, festivals, antique stores, gift shops, and even thrift shops and garage sales.

GOOD LUCK CHARMS

Many sock monkey enthusiasts believe sock monkeys bring good luck. While no one can substantiate the source of this socktastic sock monkey belief, many people believe in the charm of sock monkeys. In a world where we welcome all the luck we can receive to help offset everyday trifles and troubles, who will be the one to burst the good luck aura that seemingly surrounds our cute and collectible sock monkeys?

Stories about the charm of sock monkeys are plentiful, as everywhere sock monkeys go, they work magic to uplift spirits. People bring them to sports games as showy stalwart sports fans, to hospitals as get well gifts, to schools as learning tools, and to work to relieve stress or bond employees together. Monkeys also debut at showers, graduations, weddings, and other family events to generate well wishes. They are even sent to servicemen to help soothe homesickness.

Simply said, people view handmade sock monkeys as magical marvels—and in the very least, they spread good will wherever they go!

Only one pair of socks is required to make a traditional monkey that includes the monkey's cap.

SOCKLORE: Red-heel sock monkeys are stuffed with charm!

Family Heirlooms

Don't live life threadbare! Sock monkeys attract people of every age, class, gender, and ethnicity. Handcrafted toys that stemmed from the necessity of making inexpensive gifts for loved ones, the red-heel sock monkey today is universal in its appeal. Sock monkeys are created as gifts given to prominent people and celebrities, and to legal, medical, and business professionals.

You are never too late to jump onto the sock monkey bandwagon! A sock monkey enthusiast, 92 years young, bought a monkey for her 98 years young-at-heart sibling! Proof one is never too old to monkey around!

Monkeys created as sentimental gifts for someone's friend, co-worker, child, sibling, parent, aunt or uncle, grandparent, or loved one are the mainstay of this folk art. These soft sculpture creations, made from everyday work socks whose initial purpose was to cushion America's feet, have since taken a foothold in the world, proving that our red-heel socks mean more to us than footwear. For sock monkey crafters have *sockceeded* in lovingly creating a tradition that carries special sentimental meaning, and their sock creations are prized valuable keepsakes in today's highly disposable world.

They are *sole* mates and conversation pieces often seen peeking out of car windows, travel bags, and backpacks, amusing travelers abroad. They are the life of the party, entertaining guests as centerpieces for baby showers, birthdays, graduations, weddings, retirements, and other family festivities.

Vote for Sock Monkeys! With every sock monkey created, another ballot is cast for sock monkeys as favorite toys!

Why do so many people, from so many walks of life, share such a passion? Sock monkeys tug at the very thread of our *soles* and remind us of simple pleasures and wholesome goodness. They are cherished for the humor and levity they bring to our hectic lives. They are a gift from the heart—not a flash-in-the-pan gimmick or a fashionable trend to be exploited.

Their cheery faces bring humor and hugs to help offset stress in the workplace, at school, or at home. Their likenesses have been transferred to fabrics, clothing, cakes, and myriad other sock monkey novelty products. Simply said, sock monkeys have become part of everyday family life—they live life large as family heirlooms.

The momentum of this tradition lives on through sock monkey enthusiasts who cherish their sock monkeys from childhood and proudly pass them down within their families for generations. Well preserved or tough-loved, these heirlooms sit, lifelike, in chairs, lie on beds, or shillyshally with caregivers at places such as beaches, playgrounds, and sporting events. Their monkeyshines are often pasted into personal scrapbooks or added to blogs and websites where they are immortalized by care-givers who are not shy about their bragging rights.

With each passing year, the silly antics of sock monkeys attract newbies who have caught onto sock monkey mania. These fresh-starts step into the world of *sockmonkeydom* and unwittingly accept the baton to uphold the red-heel sock monkey tradition, so weaving the threads of our coveted sock monkeys as family heirlooms into the next generation and beyond.

Just as we name our family pets, we often lovingly name our sock monkeys with catchy, sweet, or silly monkey monikers. Personalized with family member attributes such as eye and hair colors, and dressed in garments made from family clothing or outfits that represent occupations or interests, they quickly become priceless family keepsakes.

Hot Collectibles

Funky, unconventionally stylish sock monkeys are not only fun to create, but these wild and wacky monkeys are also fun to collect! Handmade, soft sculptured, red-heel sock monkeys, with their unique characteristics, are highly sought by sock monkey collectors. If you are on the trail of a hot monkey tail to create or add to your collection, and don't want to take a sock-soaking, this chapter and section II of this book are must-reads!

Handcrafted red-heel sock monkeys with one-of-a-kind features often outshine mass-produced sock monkeys that possess no differentiating characteristics.

MONK-O-METER MONEY SCALE

To show the *socknormous* price nuances behind this booming sock trade, I have devised my Monk-O-Meter Money Scale to separate sock monkeys into three categories, ranking them with high, medium, and low values based on my knowledge of their general value in the marketplace.

Category values are based on prices of newly made or already-loved handmade vintage sock monkeys created from adult-size and miniature-size brown heather red-heel socks woven originally by NKC, and newly made or already-loved modern sock monkeys created from adult-size brown heather red-heel socks woven by FRM.

Vintage miniature and newly made vintage sock monkeys within any of the Monk-O-Meter Money Scale categories have been known to tip the scale!

NOTE: *Monkeys created from other colored red-heel socks manufactured by NKC (adult size in blue, gray, red/green, green/red, white, variegated blue, and miniature blue) are too rare to value. Monkeys created from other-colored red-heel socks manufactured by FRM (adult size in blue, pink, red, yellow, green, and small kid brown mini) are too new on the market to ascertain values.*

Sock monkeys fashioned from red-heel socks hand-dyed different colors are extremely rare and add to the thrill of a collector's hunt! They are a must-have for anyone looking to round out their eclectic collection. Price? "High" on the Monk-O-Meter Money Scale, or maybe even out of this world.

Each crafter has his or her own style of monkeying around, and it is this assortment of styles that attracts collectors. To obtain a wide range of different sock monkey looks in my collection, I purchase or create primarily brown and cream-colored (brown heather) handmade red-heel sock monkeys from within all three Monk-O-Meter Money Scale categories. Sock monkeys made from different colors and sizes of red-heel socks (miniature, mini, small, medium, large, or X-large) and sock monkey couples or families add even more character, good cheer, and smiles!

"High" on the Monk-O-Meter

Socktacular sock monkeys that mirror famous people and heroic personalities from storybook or comic book characters, as well as *spooktacular* monkeys that render us weak or speechless from frightful or laughable imitations of monsters and villains, are the crème de la crème of collections. Exquisite designer sock monkeys, like Socktain Hook or a beautiful bride, created with many distinctive features, typically rank high in value on the Monk-O-Meter Money Scale. Their uniqueness and the skill level required to create such detailed monkeys often make them most expensive to acquire. Fanciful sock monkey couples and sock monkey families command even more money. Few are available in the marketplace, as these labor-of-love works are typically not profitable for crafters to create and sell.

"Medium" on the Monk-O-Meter

Sockdillyumptuous sock monkeys that mimic our job occupations or special interests, and sock monkeys made to order to imitate special people in our lives, with matching eye and hair colors or other attributes, are often ranked medium to high on the Monk-O-Meter Money Scale. Such monkeys—dressed in clothes that express a profession, patriotism, or favorite sport, or festooned for special occasions or even dressed as everyday loafers—are relatively affordable, depending on embellishments, dress, accessories, and props. These sock monkeys, typically created with a few distinctive features, are fun highlights of any collection.

"Low" on the Monk-O-Meter

Sockfice it to say, sock monkeys created with basic characteristics and attributes, such as Rosebud's, can nonetheless charm anyone's socks off. Although these monkeys are lowest on the Monk-O-Meter Money Scale, do not let this ranking fool you! Sock monkey enthusiasts adore them, and these lovable, huggable monkeys represent the foundation of collections because they are the most affordable. They are plentiful in the marketplace, except around peak holiday periods.

Field training is vital if you are on a mission to obtain red-heel socks or red-heel sock monkeys from the lineage of the red-heel sock monkey tradition.

SOCK MONKEY COGNOSCENTI

Sock monkey sellers who are not the crafters of the monkeys they are selling often do not know the sock origins of the monkeys or inadvertently leave out such information in their advertisements. Before collectors make sock monkey purchases, they should ask questions to authenticate each monkey's sock origin if the traditional red-heel sock lineage is important to them.

Seasoned collectors possess more sock monkey savoir faire and can normally ascertain the authenticity of a sock monkey by simply looking at the monkey or a photograph of one and asking a few questions.

Sock monkey newbies, with little to no experience in purchasing red-heel socks or sock monkeys, can acquire an understanding of the subtle differences between socks woven by NKC and FRM by reading section II. Until novice collectors build their *sockopedia* knowledge based upon these fundamentals, they may unwittingly procure socks or monkeys from an offshoot of the lineage.

When do you know whether you have started a collection of sock monkeys? Only when I had nine sock monkeys, with "Rosebud" being the first, did I think of myself as a sock monkey collector. But collections can be small or large—even a size of one. Although my collection primarily consists of monkeys created from red-heel socks woven by NKC or FRM, other collections often include monkeys mass-produced or uniquely created from other sock sources.

Don't be shy like Fretty—ask questions!

SOCK MONKEY QUEST QUESTIONS

- Safety always comes first—does the sock monkey come with an age caution warning? Small parts may be safety hazards for pets or children under the age of four.

- If allergies are a concern, was the monkey created in a smoke- and pet-free environment?

- Will the material contents used in the making of the monkey adversely affect your health or the recipient's health, if the monkey is to be a gift?

- Will the monkey you are looking to purchase be the actual monkey you will receive, or will the seller/maker be selling you a similarly created monkey? This could make a difference if the monkey is handmade, as it could be difficult for a crafter to achieve the same look twice.

- What is the brand (origin) and color of socks used to make the monkey?

- Does the monkey have a red heel for the mouth piece AND a red heel for the bum?

- Is the monkey handmade (one-of-a-kind) or from a line of mass-produced monkeys with the same look, often termed as vanilla/manila sock monkeys?

- Does the monkey have any tags or credentials? If so, what do they say?

- What is the size of the monkey or from what size socks has the monkey been made? (See section II).

- Who is the creator/maker of the monkey? Are initials or other identification markings permanently affixed (marker, paint, or embroidered) or is there a loose or attached identification tag on the monkey?

- What is the age of the monkey? (Sometimes the type of stuffing used will help identify age.)

- Are the features of the monkey, such as eyebrows and eyelashes, embroidered, painted, or glued? (There are times when an application technique for creating features cannot be ascertained simply by looking at a photograph.)

- What is the condition of the monkey, clothes, and accessories as applicable: new, like new, well-loved, or tough-loved? If not new, is there discoloration from sun damage or washing? Are there loose threads, runs, rips, or holes? Are facial features, ears, limbs, tail, or pom-poms missing from the monkey? Are all pieces of clothing and accessories intact? Do the monkey, clothes, and accessories have an odor from mustiness, smoke, or other factors? Are there any stains?

- If applicable, are the clothing and accessories removable, sewn, or glued onto the monkey?

- If applicable, are clothing articles, such as fur, authentic or faux?

- If applicable, are accessories such as earrings, necklaces, and bracelets composed of real gems, costume jewelry, plastic, or other materials?

- Is the price of the monkey firm or negotiable, and does it include shipping, handling, insurance, or other service fees? Is the monkey returnable for a full refund?

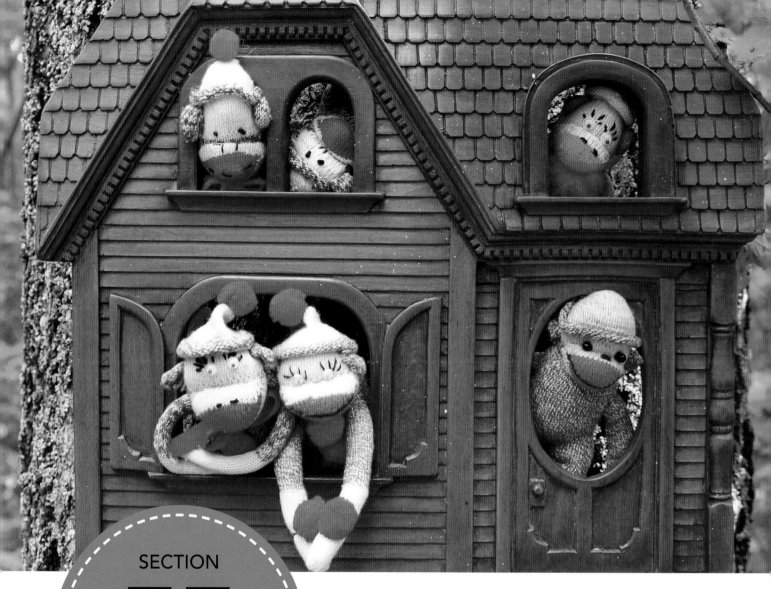

The Ins and Outs
of Monkeying
Around

Know Your Sock Seams

You can be a *sockmeister* in no time! All you need to know is in your threads! Life is full of socks, and if you buy red-heel socks not with their original packaging, it may be difficult to identify the sock brand should the origin of the socks be important to you.

The red-heel sock design trademark was registered by NKC in 1933, and from this red-heel design, sock monkeys were given their cheery red grins and colorful red bums. Sock monkeys crafted from red-heel socks manufactured by NKC and subsequently by FRM since 1992, with slight sock differences, comprise the foundation of the American red-heel sock monkey tradition.

The slight differences between the two company's red-heel socks primarily provide the basis for categorization of red-heel socks manufactured by NKC as vintage and by FRM as modern. Familiarity with socks knitted by these two companies will help crafters alleviate any *socktoesis* they may have in keeping their socks straight, and enable them to identify the resulting vintage and modern sock monkeys from this lineage.

Red-heel socks manufactured by other knitting mills have been used by crafters, but, primarily, only red-heel socks from NKC and FRM are presented herein for reference and comparison purposes.

NKC red-heel socks = Vintage
FRM red-heel socks = Modern

Socks offered in their original packaging are quite pricey and normally sought by collectors who typically do not open them. But crafty crafters, who love the fabulous differences in the sock monkeys that result from these vintage socks, will often take the pricey plunge with no regrets about opening the package of collectible socks for the sake of their art.

Sometimes, these vintage socks are sold as "seconds," or what is termed "irregulars." This means the socks have a flaw, such as a run in the knitting or some other slight irregularity. Crafters can typically hide such flaws in their creations, which maintains these socks' desirability. Be sure to ask questions about the condition of any vintage red-heel socks you may want to purchase, especially if they are not sealed in their original packaging.

NELSON KNITTING COMPANY: VINTAGE RED-HEEL SOCKS

Nelson Knitting Company (NKC) knitted blue, gray, red/green, green/red, white, variegated blue, and brown heather red-heel socks for the multitudes to enjoy. These socks are now considered rare, with only a few crafters and collectors known to have samples of many of these colorful socks in their possession.

NKC Vintage Adult-Size Red-Heel Socks

Sock monkey enthusiasts can still find NKC's adult-size brown heather red-heel socks periodically available for purchase in the marketplace. Their other colors of adult-size red-heel socks, while rarer, may be found if one diligently looks. While occurring less and less, these red-heel socks may enter the market as a result of estate or business stock liquidation sales and come unopened in their original packages or as individual unwrapped pairs.

When people uncover a small stash of NKC's worn or unused vintage socks stowed in a trunk or craft drawer by their grandmothers, they may make them available in the marketplace to sock monkey enthusiasts.

If you are not in a hurry to buy a pair of vintage NKC socks of any size, patience and diligence have their rewards. Over time, regardless of whether they are new or seconds, packaged or loose, vintage socks will likely be advertised through websites and online auctions.

NKC Vintage Miniature Red-Heel Socks

Adorable miniature vintage red-heel socks, with a height of about 5½ inches (14 cm), were sample socks knitted by NKC in blue or brown heather for use in their red-heel sock marketing campaigns. These tiny but mighty socks were often given gratis to retail outlets such as Sears and Montgomery Ward for special promotions. While infants may have worn these tiny socks, crafters fashioned them into miniature Christmas tree sock ornaments and miniature sock monkeys. These miniature red-heel socks are highly sought by crafters and collectors, but they are extremely hard to find in the marketplace. The good news: when they are offered for sale, most sellers and buyers do not seem to be aware of their rarity and they often sell below the price range of standard adult-size vintage red-heel socks. Buyers in the right place at the right time can make *sockpendous* miniature sock scoops!

FOX RIVER MILLS, INC.: MODERN RED-HEEL SOCKS

Fox River Mills (FRM) continues to delight crafters and collectors with the availability of a modern version of red-heel socks. These modern red-heel socks are common in the marketplace.

This company's red-heel socks were first offered in adult standard sizes in the color of brown heather. Currently, crafters and collectors can procure red-heel socks offered in multiple adult sizes and colors. Kid-size small socks are available in brown mini.

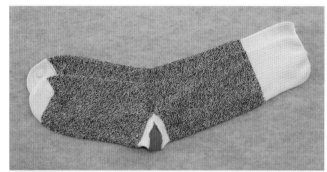

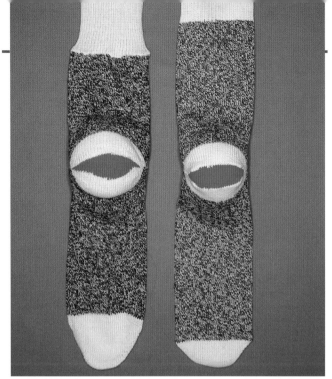

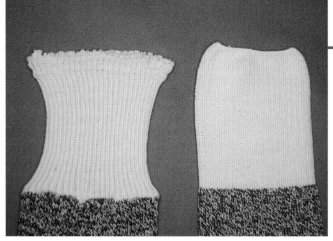

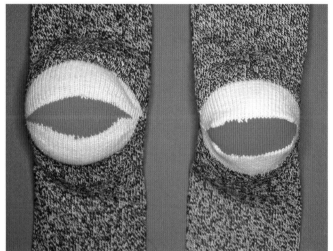

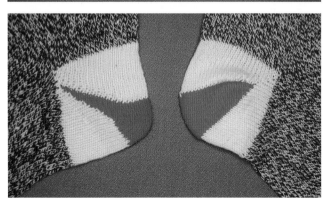

The Outside Sock Scoop—Adult Size

SEE THE DIFFERENCES

When red-heel socks are in their original packaging, there is little doubt as to the manufacturer. But when they are purchased loose, crafters or collectors need to know the slight sock differences between the vintage red-heel socks woven by NKC and the modern red-heel socks woven by FRM to ascertain the manufacturer. (Within each photograph, a vintage red-heel sock is shown on the left with a modern red-heel sock on the right.)

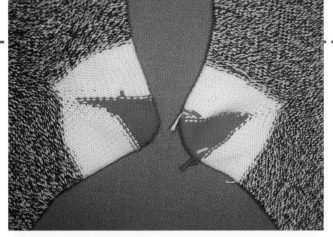

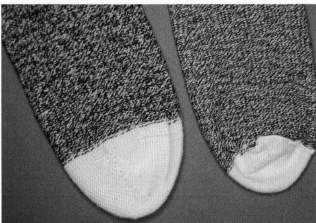

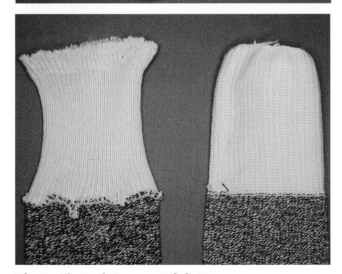

The Inside Sock Scoop—Adult Size

READ THE DIFFERENCES

NKC

- Upswing to edges of red color in the red-heel area
- Larger cream-colored area surrounding red-heel area
- Larger cream-colored area in toe area
- Inside seam differences

FRM

- Elongated oval for red color in the red-heel area
- Smaller cream-colored area surrounding red-heel area
- Smaller cream-colored area in toe area
- Inside seam differences

NOTE: *For more details about the differences between socks, packaging, and care, see page 160.*

RED-HEEL SOCK SIZE AND COLOR SCOOP

Size Scoop

If you want to create sock monkeys of various sizes, learn what size sock creates what size monkey. The following chart is offered as a guide, with approximate sock monkey heights derived primarily by measuring from the top of the head to the bottom of the foot. Different stuffing amounts and seam allowances could alter heights. Should a family of sock monkeys be on your create list, each sock size has also been correlated to give a family perspective.

Color Scoop

Colors of red-heel socks and their availability influence sock monkey making—and color choices are plentiful when one considers *sockfoolery* abounds beyond the colors introduced by NKC and FRM in the marketplace.

NKC: Adult-size red-heel socks in blue, gray, red/green, green/red, white, variegated blue, and brown heather
Miniature-size red-heel socks in blue and brown heather
FRM: Adult-size red-heel socks in blue, pink, red, yellow, green, and brown heather
Kid-size small red-heel socks in brown mini

Crafters know no limits and will go to great lengths to create monkeys from a rainbow of colors. They have raised the monkey bar by dyeing red-heel socks to colors of their choice—even bleaching socks when they want to create *spooktacular* sock monkeys, or ones from another dimension.

SOCKS (ONE PAIR)	ESTIMATED SOCK MONKEY SIZES	BRAND
Size Miniature	5"–6" (12.7–15.2 cm) "infant" sock monkey	NKC
Size Kids' SM	7½"–8½" (19–21.6 cm) "toddler" sock monkey	FRM
Size Adult S	16" (40.6 cm) "child" sock monkey	NKC and FRM
Size Adult M	18" (45.7 cm) "teen/petite adult" sock monkey	NKC and FRM
Size Adult L	20" (50.8 cm) "average adult" sock monkey	NKC and FRM
Size Adult XL	22" (55.9 cm) "large adult" sock monkey	NKC and FRM

Know Your Monkey Faces

To visualize what a vintage or modern red-heel sock monkey looks like from the folds of socks shown in chapter 5 is difficult for even the most creative of crafters! Crafters with little to no experience distinquishing between the finished looks that result from the two styles of socks when fashioned into sock monkeys will gain experience as their differences are revealed in photographs herein.

Once you see the vintage and modern red-heel sock monkeys created from this red-heel sock lineage, you can decide with positive *sockitude* whether you prefer to create or collect vintage, modern, or maybe both styles of threads.

Cute and collectible sock monkeys, handcrafted from either vintage or modern red-heel socks and enlivened with myriad faces—silly, sweet, and sassy—comprise the red-heel sock monkey tradition, which is always a creative work in progress.

To help you make sock monkey sense of the two companies' red-heel socks, study and compare the photographs herein and apply what you learned in chapter 5 about the red-heel sock lineage differences. These differences, when applied to the vintage and modern red-heel sock monkeys, will be apparent by the attributes of their heads, colorful smiles, and red bums.

The marketplace primarily offers red-heel sock monkeys, ranging in height from 2 inches (5.1 cm) to 4 feet (122 cm), that are not of the NKC and FRM red-heel sock lineage. If you are shopping for monkeys, be sure to ask questions if this lineage is important to you.

My pal is vintage and I'm modern.

NKC Standard Size

NELSON KNITTING COMPANY: VINTAGE RED-HEEL SOCK MONKEYS

Miniature Size

Miniature red-heel vintage sock monkeys created from tiny, vintage NKC socks need few words. If you ever cradle a miniature monkey in your hand, you will be *sockitized* by its magic. Even though their sculpted bodies are only about 5½ inches (14 cm) tall (depending on stuffing and seam allowance), they can easily take as long to make as the standard-size monkeys. From personal experience, miniature monkeys are extremely difficult to create because of their tiny parts, but the mojo they spread is well worth the effort. Miniature vintage red-heel socks and miniature monkey sightings are rare in the marketplace, but your hunt for them will be well rewarded if you are on mini-monkey alert and find one or more. This size monkey makes for a great compact travel companion!

Miniature brown heather sock monkeys are difficult to find. And while miniature blue socks were manufactured by NKC, I have only seen one pair in this color and have yet to behold a miniature blue sock monkey.

NKC miniatures reel in a bunch of fun!

FOX RIVER MILLS, INC.: MODERN RED-HEEL SOCK MONKEYS
FRM Standard Size

Kids' Size Small

Sock monkeys made from FRM's modern kid-size small red-heel socks can be found in the marketplace, but availability of these sock monkeys is not yet seen in large numbers. Like monkeys created from NKC's miniature-size socks, this size monkey, which ranges in height from 7½ to 8½ inches (19 to 21.6 cm), makes a great travel companion.

READ THE DIFFERENCES!

The slight differences between standard-size red-heel sock monkeys from the NKC and FRM red-heel sock lineage are usually easy to spot.

- Eyes of vintage sock monkeys are typically sewn within the cream-colored toe area. Since the cream-colored toe area of modern socks is smaller, modern monkeys' eyes are commonly placed within the brown-colored area bordering the cream-colored toe area.

- Edges of the red heel of vintage sock monkeys swing up or down. The red heel of modern sock monkeys are elongated red ovals. Since two matching socks (one pair) are typically used to create one monkey, both the monkey's sunny smile and nether regions, from which the monkey flamboyantly "moons" the world should match.

- The texture of vintage verses modern sock monkeys is different, but extremely difficult to ascertain unless one has unworn, unwashed pairs of socks from both companies with which to compare the texture of the monkey in question. If the monkey has been aged by the sun, used, or washed, this comparison becomes almost impossible. As material contents of red-heel socks change, it becomes more complex to ascertain a sock monkey's lineage in this way.

Crafty techniques used by crafters to alter the shape or the color of red-heel socks may further make identification of vintage or modern monkeys difficult. For instance, crafters may:

- Embroider upswings into the elongated red-heel ovals of modern sock monkeys using matching red embroidery thread.
- Reshape red-heel smiles.
- Dye or bleach red-heel socks from original colors to ones of their choice.

Feel the Differences!

While not easily done, sock differences can sometimes be assessed by sock texture, as material content between the two types of socks differs (See page 160). Also, vintage monkeys were often stuffed with textiles like nylons or Kapok. Today's monkeys are typically stuffed with fiberfill, making these monkeys lighter in weight.

Test time! Three images of sweet, handmade sock monkeys are shown here. Can you guess from which socks they were created? Answers clockwise from right: NKC, FRM, another red-heel sock source. Sock monkeys created from socks of other red-heel sock manufacturers are plentiful and there is usually a sock monkey maker and collector for each and all, no matter the lineage.

Dexter has all the monkey moves, and so can you!

Getting Ready to Monkey Around

CHAPTER 7

Do You Have the Sewing Skills?

An adult with basic sewing skills, or a child who is under the guidance and supervision of an adult who has these skills, will be able to create a handmade, one-of-a kind, basic red-heel sock monkey. Optional distinctive features and quick-fix sock monkey clothes made sock monkey style can also be created, but may require additional skills.

BASIC SEWING SKILLS REQUIRED

- Awareness of how to safely handle scissors, sewing needles, and small items such as buttons.
- Ability to read, comprehend, and apply easy instructions and diagrams to enable you to cut, piece, shape, and sew together various sock parts into the shape of a sock monkey.
- Finger dexterity to turn sock pieces inside-out and right-side out again.
- Ability to sew whip stitches, straight running stitches, or backstitches.
- Knowledge of how to reinforce start and end points of seams.
- Ability to tie off thread ends (knots).

OPTIONAL SEWING SKILLS

- Ability to machine-sew long seams or other parts of a sock monkey. (Basic hand sewing skills will still be required to complete the sock monkey.)
- Ability to sew gather stitches, satin stitches, and French knots if the sewer wants to create a sock monkey with certain distinctive features.

KEEP SAFETY IN MIND

Be responsible! Always think of safety first when you create a sock monkey.

Know how to handle scissors, needles, dust sprays, irons, and other items you want to use. Ask someone who is in the know to help if you are unsure of processes and products. Wear a filter mask to keep dust and other particles out of your lungs when you cut, sew, and stuff your sock monkey. Avoid the use of toxic paints, glue, and other harmful materials. Use allergy-free fiberfill for stuffing, and work in a pet- and smoke-free area.

If you help someone with limited sewing skills make a sock monkey, make the sewing project fun for both of you and instill a sense of pride and accomplishment at the same time. With safety foremost, teach the other person how to sew one or more monkey parts, or obtain the other person's input about the look of the sock monkey to include them in the creative process.

CAUTION: Only create a sock monkey for someone who is four years old or older as small parts could cause a choking hazard. Do not give a sock monkey with small parts to a child or pet.

Do You Have Time and Motivation?

When heartfelt creative impulses stir your *sole,* listen to this inner calling—this momentum is a gift! Don't ignore how you feel. Let the sock monkey mojo in you take hold and get busy monkeying around!

TIME

If you are in the mood to monkey around, what are you waiting for? An undressed sock monkey can typically be created in one sitting if you have about three hours of time and use a sewing machine to sew parts with long seams, sewing other parts by hand. Your monkey will take a bit longer to complete if you hand-sew the entire monkey. If you do not have this block of time available, then sew your monkey piecemeal and make your monkey a project of the week or month.

If you do not have the impetus to sew on your own, or your time is not your own, there are a number of ways to let your sock monkey mojo shine through like Squiggy's:

- Gather with other crafters for encouragement. Whether you meet in the comfort of someone's home or another safe, fun setting, small talk, chatter, and laughter make the time seemingly go by faster as each of you sews a monkey.

- Pass a sock monkey to family members or friends during the creation process to add their personal embellishments. Until the last person finishes the final stitch, no one knows how your monkey will look!

Monkey around in stages if need be, for there is no sock monkey patrol to tell you to quickly put a sock-in-it or to toe-a-timeline!

What is the secret ingredient to monkeying around? Sock monkey mojo!

- Start a sock monkey chain. Do you have several web, blog, or pen pals you have never met, but want to include them in the makings of a monkey? Imagine the fun to be had when everyone claims to be the "monkey's uncle!"

Still no time? Still no excuses! You could buy a ready-to-love sock monkey—new or already hugged. Personalize the monkey with clothing and accessories of your choice when you have time to make the monkey special to you—or ask someone else to do this. Or if you are the kind of person who just does not have time to do anything crafty, then barter with a friend or family member to create a monkey for you or gift you one!

Each handmade sock monkey is created with stitches from the heart, and when given from the heart, a monkey is a great gift of one's self that says "I care about you" to family, friends, or others.

MOTIVATION

Crafters who are up to the artistic pastime of making monkeys are plentiful. Sock monkey mojo moves them to create these prized monkeys to subsidize their budgets or to give themselves a purpose when one is needed. Others make them because they enjoy the creative process. But the biggest reason why someone sews a monkey is love!

Do You Have the Basic Tools and Supplies?

An undressed, standard-size red-heel sock monkey with basic features can be created with only a few sock monkey essentials. To create a sock monkey with distinctive features, additional supplies and skills may be necessary. Whether you create a basic or a distinctive sock monkey, all of them steal hearts! Review section IV in its entirety to identify sock monkey attributes that will knock your socks off before you make tool and supply purchases. If you want to create a simple but stunning sock monkey wardrobe—sock monkey style—clothes and accessories are discussed in section VI.

BASIC TOOLS AND SUPPLIES REQUIRED

- Pencil to sketch your monkey and scribble *sockadoodle* notes.

- One pair of red-heel socks to create one monkey.

- Sock monkey pattern instructions (see pages 136 to 141).

- Two matching buttons or other materials for eyes.

- Sharp scissors.

- All-purpose cream-colored spooled thread and sharp general-purpose needle for hand-sewing monkey parts.

- Skein of black or brown embroidery thread (six-ply strands) and embroidery needle, with a long needle eye to hand-sew button eyes onto your monkey. If you want to add upswing smiles, smile lines, eyelashes, eyebrows, satin eyes, or other basic or distinctive features made from embroidery thread, separate the six-ply strands into two sets of three strands. Some features look great with all six-ply strands used, and other features look best with only two or three strands, depending on the look you want.

- Premade pom-poms or, if handmade pom-poms are preferred, a skein or ball of washable acrylic yarn and a pom-pom making tool, whether store-bought or home-devised.

- Blunt-end rod about 9 to 12 inches (23 to 30.5 cm) long for use in stuffing fiber into hard-to-reach sock parts.
- Fiberfill or material scraps cut into ¼-by ¼-inch (6-by 6-mm) pieces. If non-allergenic, washable fiberfill is used, about 8 ounces (224 g) or more of fiberfill will firmly stuff one large standard-size sock monkey. Using less stuffing will create a softer stuffed sock monkey.

OPTIONAL TOOLS AND SUPPLIES

- Additional socks. Families of sock monkeys look best when created with different sizes of socks to depict infants to adults of various ages and girths.
- Safety filter mask. If you have allergies or want protection from airborne fibers while working with socks or stuffing, wear a painter's or other air filter mask to keep dust and other particles out of your lungs.
- Sewing machine. Certain parts of a sock monkey, such as long seams, can quickly be sewn by machine versus by hand. A universal size 14 needle is recommended, but you can use a ballpoint size 14 needle if the universal needle skips stitches while sewing a sample scrap of the sock.
- Dust remover. Use a feather duster/brush or a spray can of compressed air to remove loose sock and stuffing fibers (lint) from your sewing machine and work area.
- Nontoxic, washable, permanent fabric glue or hot glue with hot glue gun. Use these to add features onto your sock monkey such as eyes, eyebrows, and hair rather than sew, paint, or use markers for such features.
- Nontoxic, washable permanent marker; fabric pen; or craft/artist paint. Apply using a tube or a tiny paintbrush to add facial features, fingernails, or tattoos to your monkey.

- Embroidered designs; stick-on designs; or iron-on appliqués, letters, numbers, or images. Iron-on images will require the safe use of an iron with the heat setting selection set per the iron-on instructions and a protected hard surface such as an ironing board.
- A darner needle—a long needle with a large needle eye—to hand-sew the ends of handmade pom-pom ties onto your monkey's limbs, body, and/or cap, or to help secure and lace distinctive features, such as monkey booties and other trim made with yarn, shoelaces, ribbons, string, or other thick threads.
- A heavy needle, such as an upholstery needle, that will not break or bend to effortlessly sew distinctive features such as thick faux hair onto your monkey's head. However, a sewing needle with a larger shank (equating to a stronger needle for heavy work) can be used for this effort. The use of a thimble is highly recommended while doing this type of work to prevent sewing-finger soreness.
- A milliner embroidery needle works best if the French knot technique is frequently used to create distinctive features such as beauty marks. A sewing needle with a large shank will work well, too, as long as the needle eye can hold thicker thread such as embroidery thread.
- Colorful yarn or other lacework for distinctive features such as in "Booty Up" (pages 118 and 119) or to add lace trim to your monkey's cuffs with a darning needle.

A sewing machine is optional because the **entire sock monkey can be sewn by hand if desired.**

Think small and see only socks.
Think big and see a sock monkey.
Think larger than life and see a sole mate.

SECTION

IV

The Art of
Monkeying Around

Sock Monkey Characteristics

The art of monkeying around is all about creating your ideal sock monkey—a monkey with *sockitude* for you or someone else to love. As your monkey's creator, you should derive personal satisfaction upon its completion. After all, you are putting your heart and *sole* into its making, so why shouldn't you make a monkey that rocks your socks?

Forget about making tedious, perfect stitches, about taking measurements to make perfect seams, or about size and proportions to make your monkey perfect in symmetry. This specialty art is not about creating a perfect sock monkey—it's about creating a handmade friend with a free spirit and style. If you want a short monkey, tall monkey, fat or thin monkey, a bald monkey or even a mohawk hairstyle for your new monkey friend, so be it—sew it!

There are a *sockzillion* combinations of characteristics and features waiting at your fingertips from which to create your imagined sock monkey. With every choice you make and every stitch you take, be assured you will create a unique, one-of-a-kind, sock monkey marvel.

So throw the word "perfect" out of your *sockopedia* vocabulary while you look for ideas and inspiration among the many samples of sock monkey characteristics and features detailed in section IV. Make *sockadoodle* notes of sock monkey features that catch your eye and tug at your heart, or mix and match to come up with something totally different on your own. For added effect, think about what sock size will best suit your monkey, as sock size equates to sock monkey height and width and adds to the persona of your monkey. You truly are only limited by your imagination.

Basic Sock Monkey Features

What do most sock monkeys have in common? Their sensational basic features! Each sock monkey typically has nine basic features: eyes and eyelashes, smile line, nose, ears, neckline, body and limbs, tail, cap, and pom-poms.

There are seemingly endless ways to create basic sock monkey features, which is why each handmade sock monkey is considered unique and one-of-a-kind. Even if you are a beginning crafter, you will be able to put *sole* in your sock mate if you cover the basics in the creation of your new friend. If you are game for more *socktastic* tricks of this sock trade, be sure to check out chapter 12, "Distinctive Sock Monkey Features!"

If you use markers, fabric pens, or paint to create sock monkey features, use nontoxic, permanent, and washable products. Practice making features first on comparable woven material until you create non-blurry lines or shapes, for once such embellishments are added with marker or paint, they are normally permanent.

Brown-colored button eyes, like Nettie's (page 46), are difficult to make "pop" on a modern red-heel sock monkey if placed within the brown-colored portion of the sock. Such eyes are made noticeable by simultaneously sewing a two-hole, small, brown, flat button over a two-hole, larger, flat, white button.

EYES AND EYELASHES

Sock monkey eyes are the windows to their *soles* and therefore deserve arty thoughtfulness in their creation. Often considered the most compelling feature of a sock monkey, the eyes express a certain attitude, and when combined with eyelashes, emphasize countenance and even gender. Choosing the composition, color, shape, size, and placement of your monkey's eyes and eyelash accents are the most important decisions you will make in monkey crafting.

Eyes

A sock monkey's eyes are typically the first facial characteristic other people notice, and eye contact between them and your monkey's eyes will form a lasting impression. If you make monkeys for money, make sure your monkey's "a-peer-ance" makes a favorable first impression, as an eye disconnect may break a sale if your monkey's eyes do not speak to the heart of your buyer.

If eyes are sewn on they are usually added before stuffing the main body. Eyes made from material such as felt or foam sheet are whipstitched on with all-purpose thread. Eyes that are satin stitched, are added with embroidery thread.

For "eye-opening" ideas, check out the many expressive eyes of sock monkeys among the photographs of this book, the eye and eyelash illustrations on page 161, and the tips about eyes and eyelashes. Then experiment with various eye and eyelash concepts on paper in chapter 13 to give your monkey the appearance and expression you want to convey.

Most crafters position their monkey's peepers to look straight back at them, but many coy or comical expressions can be achieved, like Screwballinsky's, if positioned otherwise.

Eye Material Composition

Black or brown embroidered satin-stitched eyes, round shank buttons, and two-hole or four-hole round buttons were often used by sock monkey crafters in the past to create single layer eyes. Today's crafters often create double layers to emulate a pupil and an iris, and do so in colors similar to eyes of the monkey's intended caregiver. To achieve this look, crafters mix and match a double layer of complementing eye materials. For example, beads are placed over buttons, buttons placed over felt, felt over felt, and so on. To quickly add eye dazzle, crafty crafters simply place a smaller button on top of a larger button of a different color. This works particularly well for a modern sock monkey like Nettie whose eyes "pop" against the brown portion of the sock.

Crafters can apply monkey eyes in **different eye-catching material compositions, colors, shapes, and sizes:**

- Google/wiggly eyes
- Felt eyes
- Button eyes (flat or short shank)
- Button eyes with painted pupil or gleam accents
- Ornate or specialty button eyes
- Embroidered eyes
- Foam sheet eyes
- Fabric paint for eyes (permanent/washable/ nontoxic)
- Marker for eyes (permanent/washable/nontoxic)
- Artificial doll or animal eyes
- Bead eyes
- Eye appliqués
- Polymer clay eyes
- Other

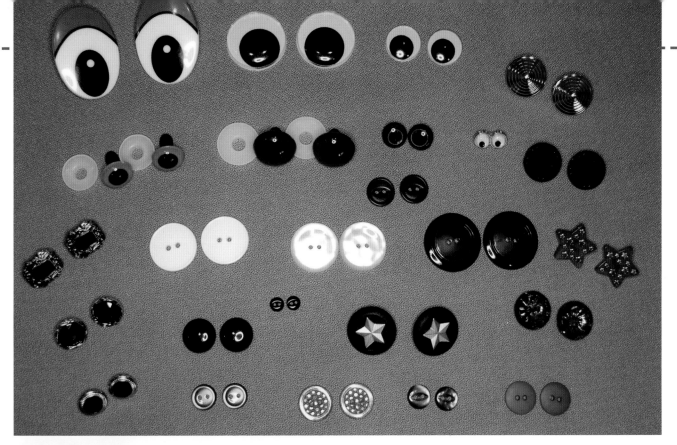

If you want to use more than one eye layer, mix and match double layers—even triple layers—of like and different eye composition material to identify the expression-filled eyes for your monkey.

Flat buttons have two or four holes and lay safely flat on material. If you want to use shank buttons for eyes, look for ones with short shanks so your monkey's eyes lie close to the sock fabric when sewn onto your monkey. Long shank buttons could get worn from jutting outward or accidentally torn off your monkey's face.

If your monkey is to wear glasses, the placement of the monkey's eyes in relation to the monkey's ears will be important. Careful placement will let your monkey's eyes "see" the world, while the temples of the glasses rest naturally over its ears.

Eye Shape and Size

Sock monkey eyes exaggerated in size to show the whites in elongated, oval, and other comical ways add a dimension of boldness or whimsy. Experiment to find whether your sock monkey's persona will shine best with beady little eyes, bloodshot eyes, large eyes of quizzical wonder, or something other. See an array of eye design ideas on page 161.

Compelling eye shapes and sizes are fun to explore. Eyes can be created from a *sockorama* of easy-to-use materials, such as foam sheet, fabric paint, felt, embroidery thread, or even polymer clay. Shapes that spoof human eyes add a realistic look.

Eye Separation and Position

Experiment with the distance between your sock monkey's eyes and the positioning of the eyes up or down in relation to the brown- or cream-colored areas of the sock. This distance and positioning can alter the look of your monkey. Give the eye distance special attention if you are going to add goggles, reading glasses, or sunglasses later.

Tip

Use embroidery thread to match the color of eye material and avoid eye-stopping visual speed bumps. Marmalade's brown button eyes were sewn with brown embroidery thread.

Eye Thread Color

The color of thread used to sew on your sock monkey's eyes can make a subtle difference. Buttons with two or four holes can be sewn on with different or matching embroidery thread. Using matching or contrasting thread colors can easily change the look of your monkey's expression, so be sure to explore this concept. If brown or black embroidery thread is used to sew on eyes, the same color can also be used to embroider eyelashes, eyebrows, or other features should color continuity be desired.

Eye Accents

If you want a "gleam" in your sock monkey's eyes, brush a smidge of white paint onto eyes of buttons or felt, sew a stitch or two of white embroidery thread onto felt or embroidered satin-stitched eyes, or glue a triangular piece of felt onto felt eyes. Practice, as the placement of an accent will create different looks! "Gleams" are usually cream or white in color. Add gleams with embroidery thread at the time you are sewing on your monkey's eyes. Add painted or glued gleams after the eyes are sewn or glued onto your monkey.

Eyelashes

A simple stitch made with emboidery thread here and there can accent a sock monkey's eyes and add more character to a sock monkey's persona. Eyelash accents enhance eyes to be more childlike and inquisitive, dreamy and demure, bold and brassy, even geeky or *spooktacular*. They are also added as a substitute for eyes when "winkers" and "sleepers" are desired.

The lengths of eyelashes play an important role in conveying the gender of your sock monkey. Most times, long eyelashes are the telltale features for female monkeys and short or no eyelashes are features of male monkeys. Medium eyelash lengths are often viewed as generic or unisex and stubby eyelashes that contour around the eyes are viewed as childlike. (See eyelash designs on page 161.)

> ## Tip
> Crafters can forgo eyelashes on a male sock monkey and add eyebrows instead to achieve a masculine look, like Sockey Jones. (See page 164 on how to create distinctive eyebrow features.)

Eyes sell! Customers will often spend fifteen minutes or more discussing whether a specific monkey is female or male before they make a purchase.

False eyelashes are a showstopper! See chapter 12 if you want to explore this distinctive feature.

Basic eyelashes can be created from embroidery thread, marker, or fabric paint. If you want embroidered eyelashes on your monkey, eyelash stitches are normally sewn before the main body is stuffed. If you want to use markers or paints to create eyelashes, apply them after the main body is stuffed. For a seamless eyelash appearance, create the eyelashes first, and add the monkey's eyes afterward to cover the lash start points.

Experiment by positioning a loose piece of embroidery thread of different lengths in different places over the red heel to identify the wondrous smile of your sock monkey friend. Try crooked, curvy, straight, and circular lines. Extend the smile line beyond the redheel area for even more variations. If you want to add a tongue, review distinctive tongue features in chapter 12 before you decide on a smile line.

SMILE LINES

Sock monkeys often take center stage and stand out in a crowd. What is the secret behind their success? Smile lines. The Smiles illustration on page 162 shows a sampling of many ways to create your monkey's special "attitude," or better said in sock monkey vernacular, your monkey's *sockitude*. Do you want your monkey to look gung-ho, happy, astounded, wily, or down-in-its-socks? Look beyond the matrix and think of the charismatic smiles or villainous grimaces of comic and animated characters illustrated in comic books, cartoons, newspapers, and on television—or look in a mirror and make your own monkey faces for fun-filled inspiration!

Whether you want a monkey smile to induce shrills, shrieks, or miles of smiles, the smile line of your choice can be applied with embroidery thread, paint, marker, rickrack, or some other material. To sew a natural-looking smile, use two- or three-ply strands of embroidery thread. Use six-ply strands of embroidery thread to sew a heavy smile line to exaggerate your sock monkey's persona. The same effects can be created with paints or markers.

Smile lines are typically brown, black, or white in color and can be solid lines or dashed. Backstitches are used to sew solid lines, and running stitches are used for dashed lines.

Sewn smile lines are usually added before the mouth piece is stuffed, and smiles applied with paint, marker, or glue are normally added after the mouth piece is stuffed and sewn onto the stuffed main body of the monkey.

Since smile lines are key in creating your monkey's mojo, explore this feature until you are smiled out. You will find there is a picture-perfect smile in the offering, just right for your ideal creation!

If you want a quick and easy smile line like Beanie Benny's, double knot the end of a three-ply strand of embroidery thread and tuck one stitch under the surface of the sock. Bring the stitch up and out about ¼ or ½ inch (6 or 13 mm) away from where the knot lies, and then swing the thread over to the other side of the smile. Tuck one stitch under the surface of the sock and bring the needle up and out ¼ or ½ inch (6 or 13 mm) away from where you want the knot to lie. Tie a double knot and snip excess thread away. You can hide the end knots by pushing the knots under the surface of the sock or leave the knots above the sock surface like Beanie Benny's.

Tips

If you do not see a smile line technique funky enough for your monkey, opt for something avant-garde! Glue a length of rickrack or other flashy trim onto your monkey's mouth piece and say "cheese!"

If you are thinking of adding a moustache to your monkey, be sure to leave space for the moustache between where you place the nose and the red-heel mouth of the monkey.

Nose, nose, anything goes! Noses can dip into the red area of your monkey's mouth piece and look perfectly at home.

NOSES

I could say sewing sock monkey noses is a draining experience and if you are not careful, you can blow it! I could run on and say sewing noses correctly is nothing to sneeze at and that would be the long and short of it. But the truth is, noses are "snot" hard to create! They are one of the easiest features crafters can pick to add to their sock monkey, and yet, they are a feature that is sometimes overlooked.

Noses can be sewn using various stitch work. See chapter 14 for how to sew the tiniest of noses with French knots or a sizable nose with a satin stitch. Sewn noses are typically added with embroidery thread before the mouth piece is stuffed, while noses applied with paint, marker, or glue are normally added after the mouth piece is stuffed and sewn onto the stuffed main body.

Check over the sampler of hand-picked noses in the Noses illustration on page 163 and promise to pick a nose, for this will be the first time you can pick your friend's nose and not be in bad taste!

Sock monkey noses can vary in size, shape, prominence, and placement. A "cute-as-a-button" nose is a simple feature easily added to your monkey. Crafters who want a nose befitting a king of apes can explore artificial animal noses. Noses are often embroidered within the cream-colored area above the red heel with three-ply strands of embroidery thread before the mouth piece is stuffed. Noses applied with paint, marker, or glue are typically added after the red-heel mouth piece is stuffed and sewn onto the main body.

EARS

The secret is out! Sock monkeys "hear no evil, see no evil, and speak no evil!" They are not sensitive to jokes about big ears, flaring ears, hairy ears, and well, you get the picture! So, if you want your sock monkey to be "all ears"—go for it!

Any size or style of ear looks befitting on a sock monkey—the more exaggerated the feature, the more grins and giggles. As with any sock monkey feature, if you can imagine it, you can create it.

Sock monkey ears can be of many shapes and sizes, and whether you want them to be small and rounded, elfin and pointed, scanty or stuffed full, your fingers can create that look. You are only limited by the amount of sock you dedicate to creating monkey ears, because unless you have a spare sock to use for a special set of jumbo-size ears, you typically can only create small to moderate-size ears without altering the sock monkey pattern and dedicating less fabric to other sock monkey parts and more fabric to ears.

Ears are sewn onto a sock monkey after the eyes are added, the main body is stuffed, and the mouth piece is sewn on.

Some glasses have bendable temples, while others do not bend. Either way, safely secure the temples of the glasses onto the sides of your monkey's head with a few overlapping whipstitches behind each of the ears so the stitches are not noticeable from a frontal view of your monkey.

If you want your sock monkey to wear an earring or two, see pages 78 to 83 for additional ideas about how to create distinctive ears beyond the basics and add a bigger pop with earring bling!

Ears usually appear on monkeys with the right side of the sock material facing out (like the rest of the body and body parts), but ears can be sewn wrong side out as a contrast to the main body.

HOW TO MAKE BASIC EARS

1. Fold one piece of the ear sock material inside out with right sides together.

2. With cream-colored thread, use a small running stitch, backstitch, or machine stitch to sew the folded material together to form the ear shape. Do not sew closed the side of the ear to be sewn to the monkey's head.

3. Trim the seam excess within ¼ inch (6 mm) of the sewn ear shape.

4. Turn the sock material right side out.

5. Stuff the ear (if desired). Fold in the raw edges of material at the open ear end. Whipstitch the ear closed.

6. Whipstitch the ear onto the monkey's head in the desired position.

7. Create the second ear, of equal size, the same way.

NOTE: *Use a double strand of all-purpose thread in the needle*

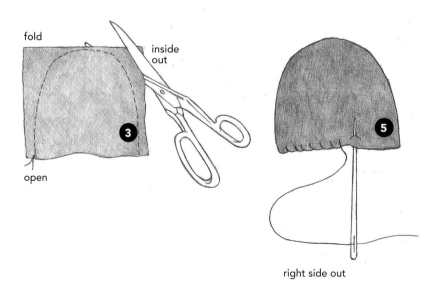

fold

inside out

3

open

5

right side out

A pair of basic sock monkey ears can easily be created, but the placement of the ears on your monkey can be tricky. A slight shift of the ears, up or down, forward or backward, on the sides of the monkey's head can change your monkey's character. If you want your monkey to seemingly peer through the lenses of goggles, reading glasses, or sunglasses, it is best to have the actual glasses your monkey will wear on hand. See where the temples of the glasses might comfortably lie on or around your monkey's ears and let the results of this "fitting" guide you to where you place the ears.

How to Make Basic Necklines

- Loosely tie yarn, ribbon, chain, or other item(s) around the neck so the natural thickness of the neck circumference remains unaltered. Or simply leave the neckline natural for a muscular or masculine look.

NECKLINES

When you think about your sock monkey's persona, don't forget to give special consideration to a befitting neckline, as a sock monkey's neck size is a feature that often emphasizes girth, gender, or childlike characteristics. The circumference of your monkey's neckline can be effortlessly altered after your sock monkey is completely sewn.

If you have already chosen the clothes your sock monkey will wear, or you plan to dress your sock monkey later, you may need to make neckline adjustments to the clothing or to your monkey's neck if the outfits have collars or other neck-fitting closures.

No clothes planned? Not a worry—choose a neckline accessory that will make a simple statement on its own!

- Pull, tighten, and secure yarn or other decorative neck accessories around the neckline to reduce neck size if a dainty, demure, or large-headed child-like look, or simply a smaller neck size, is desired.

- Move the neck accessory up or down along the neckline to create different looks, like the twins Inky and Dinky. Experiment with the placement and tightening of the accessory before you securely tie off the item.

BODY AND LIMBS

Psst . . . Want in on a little secret? The embellishment of your sock monkey's main body and limbs is often the most overlooked feature that can enhance your sock monkey's persona. So now that the secret is out, take time to think about what kind of body would enrich your monkey's perceived character. Stuffing density, length of limbs, placement of limbs, and other body attributes should be addressed before your monkey's main body and limbs are sewn and stuffed.

Stuffing Density

Most sock monkeys keep their body shape for years if they are stuffed firmly. Other monkeys, stuffed with less filling, may lose their intended shape after a few months of hugs. How you want your monkey to feel in your or someone else's arms is up to you!

Monkeys with less stuffing make soft and cuddly bodies, perfect for bed pillow companions, and they can be posed in endearing positions like Mopey, aka Hammy. Firmly stuffed bodies make stout monkeys, great for active play friends. An overstuffed body can make a monkey look fat, short, and chunky—maybe even a bit hunky! A less stuffed body can make a monkey look skinny—and skinny monkeys often look tall. However, keep in mind that an understuffed monkey may look gaunt or lifeless. Of course, there are myriad variations in between.

How firm should your monkey's main body and other parts be? You will know the answer when you begin to stuff your monkey, as it is all about your interpretation of what your sock monkey should be.

Exaggerated Body and Limbs

Besides putting life into your sock monkey's body through stuffing, you can also enhance or exaggerate your monkey's body and limbs through sock foolery! If you want to shorten arms or legs, sew them smaller in size when you sew their seams. If you want to make arms or legs look thin, sew them narrow, and vice versa if you want them to be more robust.

You can make your sock monkey's arms or legs seem longer by sewing its other limbs shorter in comparison. If you want your sock monkey to have lengthy arms, sew shorter legs. For a long-legged monkey, make the arms shorter. You can also use a smaller size sock for the main body, and create arms from a larger sock.

But, before you go to extra expense for additional red-heel socks of various sizes, a nifty trick to lengthen your monkey's body and limbs is to simply add a hair piece, an extra-large hair ribbon, a hat, mittens, or shoes to whatever extremity you choose to lengthen.

> ## Tip
> To quickly add height to your sock monkey, stuff the sock cap before sewing the hat onto your monkey's head.

Hockey Sockey Puck is a favorite with sport fans—his long arms get him out of sticky situations!

Most times, the arms are sewn onto the stuffed main body of the monkey after the mouth piece, facial characteristics, and ears are sewn onto the monkey.

Other Boggling Body Shapes

While you have monkey body sizes and parts floating around in your mind, ask yourself whether your monkey needs a little something more in the way of being shapely. What about defined wrists to give your monkey more lifelike definition? Wrap and tighten cream-colored thread around the wrist area of your monkey several times and then tie off and knot your thread on the back of the wrist, trim the excess thread away, and tuck your knot below the surface of the sock fabric. It's a cinch! Or go all out with curves, biceps, slim waistlines, and more—read Shapely Secrets in chapter 12.

How and Where to Sew and Place the Arms

After you whipstitch the ends of your monkey's arms safely closed, there are two ways to sew them onto your monkey's body. Most often, the circumference of the arm is formed into a rounded shape and the circular ends are whipstitched onto the main body. An even simpler technique, but one less used by crafters, is to flatten the ends of the arms and whipstitch them flat onto the main body. Regardless of your choice, be sure to sew the arms onto your monkey so the long underarm seams face downward, hidden from view.

Also, similar to the placement of ears, experiment before you decide where to sew the arms onto the sides of your sock monkey, as a slight shift in placement of the arms up, down, forward, or backward can make a big character change. Sometimes a sock monkey appears to have a long, large neck when arms are placed low on the body. This masculine look can be a crowd-pleaser as the monkey takes on the world *monkey-a-mano*.

If your sock monkey is to wear neckline ribbons or ties, the placement of the arms is important. Be sure to leave space between the head and arms to place such accessories.

Once your magnificent sock monkey comes out of your body shop, do not be alarmed if your monkey masterpiece needs a recall in the future. Just as we sag with age, so can your monkey! Continue to fine-tune your monkey over the years with facial and body massages to perk up your monkey's sagging body parts, as unlike our bodies, their sock bodies are quite forgiving and can, most times, be easily shaped back into their original forms. Or, if you prefer, perform a total monkey makeover to completely overhaul your monkey.

TAIL

Deciding on the style of a sock monkey tail can put anyone into a tailspin, for even though the tail might be the last thing people notice, it makes a memorable impression. Fat, skinny, stubby, short, long, rounded, pointed, straight, curled, kinky, and other tails cover a broad gamut of choices crafters can explore for their sock monkey.

Your monkey's tail should exemplify, parody, or exaggerate what you have in mind for your monkey's persona. If you create an impish monkey, consider creating a pointed tail. If you want to create a flamboyant movie star, consider a long tail to accessorize with bling. Or perhaps something avant-garde like a knotted tail will fit your monkey's persona!

Experiment in your mind or on paper. Most crafters simply choose to create long straight tails to give versatility. This tail style is great for quick-change artists who want to change the mood of their monkeys instantly, as they can attach trinkets, jewelry, ribbons, pom-poms, and other showy accessories along the tail's length.

The tail is often a challenging feature, for a tail can be difficult to turn right side out after sewing the long seam, and troublesome to stuff afterward due to the tail's narrowness and sheer length. While tools exist in the marketplace to help turn long and narrow pieces right side out again, nimble fingers can get the task done.

The rewards are significant when you complete and finally sew your sock monkey's tail to its bum, for this will be the first time when your monkey's body will appear to be complete and begin to take on character! After you stuff the tail and whipstitch the end closed, just like the arms, keep the tail's round shape and whipstitch it rounded onto the body. Or flatten the upper end of the tail and whipstitch the flattened end onto the main body. Whichever you choose, ceremoniously attach your monkey's tail and see your friend come to life!

There are typically three choices of where to attach your showpiece tail. Whatever the tail placement, sew the tail onto your monkey with the long seam facing downward so it is not visible when your monkey is scampering about!

Explore different amounts of stuffing for **different levels of tail firmness. Dare to be different! One of the sweetest sock monkeys in my collection is one in which the crafter left the tail unstuffed in its natural glory, like Lazy Daisy. And don't forget, there are tailless monkeys in real life should you want to "ape" a tailless primate!**

Tail Placement

Tails are typically added to the stuffed main body of the monkey after the mouth piece, facial features, ears, and arms are sewn to the monkey.

- Center the tail in the cream-colored area above the red bum area and whipstitch the tail to the main body.
- Center the tail with part of the tail in the cream-colored area and part in the red bum area and whipstitch the tail to the main body.
- Center the tail in the red bum area and whipstitch the tail to the main body.

Tip

After the tail is stuffed and sewn onto your monkey, roll the tail forward or backward in one or more tight loops (think of rolling a garden hose), like Lil G's, and whipstitch the roll or rolls of the tail together for a cute, curled tail! Or, stuff the tail in measured amounts to create a "jointed" tail. Between each stuffed section will be a slight break in the stuffing where the tail is bendable to give an appearance of a joint or kink for pretty ribbons or ties. If you do not want any kinks in your monkey's tail, stuff the tail firmly along the entire length.

CAPS

Sock monkeys are well-known for their cheery rolled sock caps created from the cream-colored toe area of a red-heel sock and a segment of the adjoining color, like Shorty's, with enough brown-colored fabric to roll into a sock brim. Decorated with colorful tassels, pom-poms, jingle bells, or other whatnots, these sock caps have covered the heads of multitudes of monkeys over the years.

Find the front center of your sock monkey's sock cap before you add trim or sew the hat onto your monkey! Most rolled caps are placed on the monkey's head with the toe seams of the cream-colored area placed to the right and left sides of the monkey's head.

If your sock monkey will wear a rolled sock cap or other hat, your tendency may be to simply plunk the hat down on your monkey's head, but stop before you do this! There is an art to donning a hat—look at how we preen in front of our mirrors while we try them on. This preening needs to be done by you for your monkey, too! Tilt the head-wear on your monkey's head and move the hat forward, backward, and sideways to test out the many different looks. Lopsided is often a winner!

After adornment is added to your monkey's cap (see Pom-Poms in this chapter), the cap is the last part to be sewn onto your monkey. The sock cap is typically secured onto the monkey's head with intermittent, well-placed whip-stitches around the entire circumference of the cap. Many times, stuffing is added to fill out the cap's air space before the hat is secured. You can sew or glue the hat on, or leave the hat loose to easily change out when desired.

When something flashier than a traditional nappy cap is desired, here are three quick sock cap enhancements to make your monkey's headgear more stylish for today's wave of cute and collectible funky monkeys.

Lace a Brim

1. Roll the brown-colored fabric of the sock cap until it meets the cream-colored fabric of the cap.

2. Cut a 15-inch (38-cm) length of yarn.

3. Use widely spaced whipstitches to lace the yarn up through the bottom of the sock cap, around and over the rolled brim, and down again, using a large-eyed darning needle to accommodate the thicker thread, until the entire sock cap brim is laced.

4. Whipstitch the sock cap onto your monkey's head using cream-colored all-purpose thread, or keep the cap loose if desired.

Tip
If the sock cap doesn't sit and contour nicely when placed on top of your sock monkey's noggin, stuff the sock cap before sewing it onto your monkey's head. Doing so may also add some desired height to your monkey.

Trim a Brim Hat Band

1. Roll the brown-colored fabric of the sock cap until it meets the cream-colored fabric of the cap.

2. Measure the circumference of the sock cap above the rolled brim. Cut trim 1 inch (2.5 cm) larger than this measurement.

3. Overlap the ends of the trim and sew the trim ends together.

4. Place the trim to mimic a hatband around the sock cap, where the cream color of the toe and the adjoining brown color meet.

5. Secure the trim above the sock cap brim with like-colored all-purpose thread to match the primary color of the trim.

6. Sew from under the sock cap into the hatband trim, then back down inside the cap and up again, around the entire circumference, with intermittent stitches.

7. Whipstitch the sock cap onto your monkey's head using cream-colored all-purpose thread, or keep loose if desired.

You can also choose to forgo any kind of hat—all the better to display a stunning head of hair! If you envision your monkey with hair, see pages 94 to 97 for more insight before you stitch your monkey's cap on.

Tip
Don't want to sew a hatband? Glue colorful trim around the circumference of your monkey's sock cap, and then whipstitch the cap onto your monkey's head.

Make a Baseball Cap

A "quick hitter" for sports fans is to whipstitch or glue a colorful brim akin to a baseball hat to the underside of the rolled brim of your monkey's cap. A brim can be made from felt, leather, foam sheet, or other materials in favorite team colors.

1. Roll the brown-colored fabric of the sock cap until it meets the cream-colored fabric of the cap.

2. Leave the rolled sock brim natural, or lace, or mimic a hatband around the circumference of the sock cap using the technique on page 68.

3. Use the baseball brim pattern on page 165 to cut brim from foam sheet, felt, or other stiff fabric.

4. Turn the cap wrong side out. Locate the toe seams inside the cream-colored area of the cap.

5. Glue or whipstitch the baseball brim (wrong side facing you) to the inside of the cap between the toe seams where the cream and brown colors meet. If glue is used, lay a heavy weight (such as a book) over the sock cap to apply pressure until the glue is dry.

6. Turn right side out.

7. Add a pom-pom, letters, appliqués, or other hat trim garnishments as desired.

8. Whipstitch the sock cap onto your monkey's head, if desired, with a general-purpose needle, and cream-colored all-purpose thread, or keep it loose.

1

2

4

5

6

7

POM-POMS

Pom-poms are the "sunshine" in a sock monkey's *sole*. People expect to see a traditional red-heel sock monkey decked out in pom-poms, and a monkey without at least one pom-pom is like a banana split with whipped cream but with no cherry on top.

Monkeys done up in pom-pom splendor are usually adorned with six or more of these stylish staples—one on the top of their sock cap, one on each arm and leg, and one on their tails. Sometimes several small pom-

Adorn you sock monkey with pom-poms of different sizes and colors. Mix and match until you have a befitting combination! If pom-poms are not for your monkey, tie colorful string(s), laces, or yarn onto your monkey's hat and limbs and see your creation emanate life from head to toe.

To adorn a sock cap with a pompom, thread one tie end of the pom-pom onto a darning needle and draw it through to the inside of the cap. Repeat with the other tie end about ½ inch (1.3 cm) apart. Then, pull the tie ends snug, firmly knot the two ends together, and cut away the excess ends.

poms adorn their chests, running down in a single line. Monkey makers might even sew a pom-pom onto their monkey's neck or tie one around their monkey's neck as a special adornment. Fewer pom-poms are used when the monkey's persona or attire clashes with these colorful features.

So, unless you are pom-pom poor or have other ideas about how your monkey can shine, do not be stingy with your monkey's radiant attributes. Let the rays of your monkey's persona glow! Pom-poms are added to the cap before the cap is sewn onto the monkey and then to other stuffed parts of the completed monkey.

How to Make Pom-poms

If ready-made store-bought pom-poms are not desired, you can create pom-poms with a commercial pom-pom tool, using the manufacturer's instructions, or a piece of cardboard.

Cardboard Technique for Standard Size Monkeys

1. Cut a piece of stiff cardboard to the desired diameter of your pom-pom.

2. Wrap yarn from a ball or skein around the cardboard over an area of about 1 inch (2.5 cm) wide, overlapping the yarn as equally as possible within this space, until you reach the pom-pom fullness you desire. Worsted medium-weight yarn is typically wound around the cardboard 40 to 60 times for a full pom-pom look. (Wrap the yarn tightly, but loose enough to later slip the yarn loops off the cardboard.)

3. Cut the yarn after you complete your last wrap.

4. Cut another piece of yarn about 12 inches (30.5 cm) in length (from the same ball or skein of yarn). This will be the tie that keeps your pom-pom together.

5. Carefully slip all of the yarn loops off the cardboard, keeping them together as tightly as possible.

6. Wrap the 12-inch (30.5 cm) yarn tie around the center of the loops twice, pulling all the loops of yarn together as tightly as possible without breaking the tie. Knot the tie securely. Do not cut the ends of the tie.

7. Hold the yarn tie ends near the knot, and cut all of the loops. Do not cut the yarn tie.

8. Holding the tie ends near the knot, shake the pom-pom and fluff the many yarn strands with your fingers for maximum fullness.

9. Hold the tie ends near the pom-pom and snip the yarn ends with sharp scissors to create a round, eye-pleasing shape. Most pom-poms are shaped like a globe. The closer you trim the ends of your pom-pom strands to the center of where you tied all of the yarn together, the tighter the pom-pom will look. Do not cut the yarn tie.

10. Place the pom-pom at the desired location, and wrap the tie ends around your monkey's limb or tail twice.

11. Knot the tie ends under the pom-pom to blend in. Snip the tie ends to the size of the pom-pom or tie them into a bow if desired.

If you make yarn pom-poms for your monkey's limbs or tail and prefer the two tie ends to be invisible, use a darning needle to thread the tie ends through the monkey's sock surface directly below where the pom-pom is to lie and up through the fabric again about ½ inch (1.3 cm) from where you inserted the needle. Then knot the ties together, and cut the tie ends to the same length of the pom-poms.

Use this method to also sew pom-poms onto the cap, neck, and chest area, if desired.

Distinctive Sock Monkey Features

Remarkable sock monkeys always get a second look when their personae soar above others with their showy lifelike features so common to us, yet often overlooked by crafters in the sock monkey creation process. Distinctive features are rarely seen on sock monkeys, but for those crafters on the cutting edge, the employment of one or more of these features adds a sensational dimension to a sock monkey's personality and potentially more money in their pockets if they offer them for sale.

Did you know a simian monkey has a belly button and ten fingers? Adding these and other attributes to your sock monkey can be a great conversation piece. Browse this chapter for these and other endearing distinctive characteristics!

Distinctive features strengthen the characteristics crafters instill in their sock monkeys to spoof or mimic famous people, characters, friends, family, and loved ones. These features are the rage of the new generation of sock monkeys and are sure to have monkey admirers grinning and giggling by the multitudes!

The challenge is on for anyone who wants to create, beyond the basics, a cute and collectible sock monkey that will turn heads. If you are up to the fun task of raising your creative "monkey bar," fifteen distinctive features, with application techniques, are detailed in the following pages to make your monkey stand out among monkey minions!

You will be amazed at how adding one or more of these wholesome features will get applause. Whether you are crafting a sock monkey to be a hot collectible, such as the King of Sock 'n' Roll, or a monkey to swing in some-one's arms, adding realistic features goes a long way. So get your creative sock monkey mojo going, and get ready for oohs and aahs, hoots and hollers, and the reward all crafters love to hear—"I wish I had thought of that!"

BEAUTY MARKS

Imitating beauty marks, such as moles and freckles, are great ways for crafters to add endearing facial features. Even frightfully fabulous warts can be emulated on a witch or a thing that goes bump in the night to create thrills and chills! How easy is it to add these features to your monkey? Depending on the technique you choose, you will probably take longer to figure out where to place them than to actually add them! Most beauty marks look best when added in black or brown colors. Red or other colors can be used to depict ailments.

- Create French knots, like Calvin's, with thick thread, such as embroidery thread. Beauty marks made from French knots should be added before the sock monkey mouth piece is stuffed and sewn.

- Dab beauty marks onto your monkey with nontoxic permanent, washable fabric paint with a paintbrush or with a pointed, nontoxic permanent colored marker. Dabbed beauty marks can be added after the red-heel mouth piece has been stuffed and sewn.

- Tie various sizes of knots—single, double, or triple—with yarn or other thick thread onto your monkey. Then snip the loose ends close to the knot. These beauty marks can be added after the red-heel mouth piece has been stuffed and sewn.

Punctuate your lil' monkey's face or body, sweetly or eerily, to create the exact persona you aim for with removable or permanent beauty marks.

Tip
The key to making beauty marks is to practice making them in different sizes with the technique you want to use on an extra sock or similar material—before you actually add the feature to your monkey.

BELLY BUTTONS

"Innie" or "outie" belly buttons, like noses, can be "cute as a button" and yet so different from one another! A belly button on any sock monkey can bring a smile to young or old caregivers. While a glitzy belly button found on a monkey belly dancer may be an expected delight, an un-suspecting belly button, peeking out from between clothes, makes for unforeseen smiles galore.

Like everything else sock monkey-wise, do not worry about how to make the perfect belly button. A belly button is easy to create, and is added to your monkey's midriff after the main body of the sock monkey is stuffed.

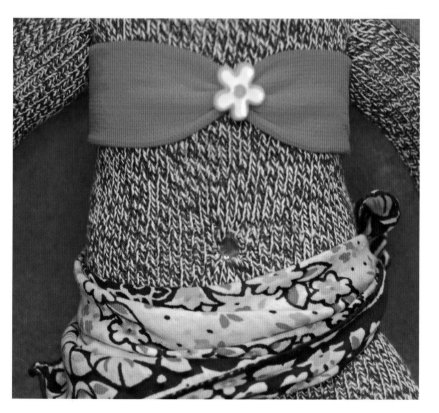

Innie Belly Button

1. Sew gather stitches with cream-colored thread in a small circle, a bit larger than the gem to be used, centered in the midriff section of the sock monkey. Do not tie off and cut the thread yet!

2. Glue a flat gem piece in place within the small circle and set the monkey aside until the glue dries.

3. Hold the gem in place with your fingers and pull the thread to the desired tightness, gathering the ma-terial snuggly around the gem.

4. Tie off the thread and snip the thread close to the knot.

5. Push the knot ends below the sock surface.

Plain or ornate buttons or gems can be sewn or glued onto your monkey's midriff.

Looking for another belly laugh? Add a belly chain around your monkey, especially if your monkey loves to lounge around in a swimsuit and you are looking to add femininity!

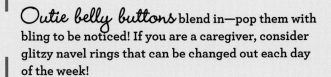

Outie belly buttons blend in—pop them with bling to be noticed! If you are a caregiver, consider glitzy navel rings that can be changed out each day of the week!

Outie Belly Button

1. Use a small piece of brown-colored sock material remnant. If a remnant of workable size (1½ by 1½ inches [3.8 by 3.8 cm]) is not available from your socks, cut about 1½ inches (3.8 cm) of brown-colored material from the base of your sock monkey's tail before you sew the tail part.

2. Roll, coil, or bunch the sock piece into a pleasing belly button shape with the material right side out to match the monkey body or wrong side out for contrast.

3. Sew the formed belly button together with cream-colored thread.

4. Tie off the thread and snip the thread close to the knot.

5. Whipstitch the belly button onto your sock monkey's midriff, tucking any unsightly edges securely under with stitches as you sew. (For additional contrast, sew the belly button onto the monkey's midriff with the belly button material going against the grain of the main body material.)

6. Tie off the thread and snip the thread close to the knot.

7. Push the knot ends below the sock surface.

"How many doubloons must a pirate give to get his ears pierced?"
ANSWER: "A-buck-an-ear, matey!"

EARS, EARS, AND MORE EARS

Now 'ear this, matey! Although your ears must be burning after reading about basic sock monkey ears in chapter 11, get ready for another all-out earful! Why? There is more to 'ear about 'em. I'm not pulling your ear—you'll soon be up to your ears with six distinctive ears beyond the basic humdrum eardrums. Perhaps these techniques will go in one ear and out the other, but they are 'ear for you to consider. Your monkey's ears can be tweaked any ol' way with your own variations, too. What you do to the space between your monkeys ears will be your, and your monkey's, little secret!

Ears are sewn onto a sock monkey after the eyes are added, the main body is stuffed, and the mouth piece is sewn on.

Tip
Hairy ears can also add great humor to your monkey. Sew or glue faux fur to your sock monkey's ears after they are sewn in place so you'll be sure to place the ear hair just right.

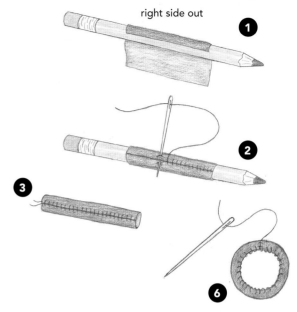

Loop Ears

1. Wrap and overlap ear material right side out around a pencil or long rod.
2. With cream-colored thread, whipstitch the length of material together along the pencil.
3. Slip the pencil out from the material.
4. Fold in the raw edges at both ends.
5. Whipstitch the ends closed.
6. Loop the material into a circle shape with the seam inside the circle, and sew both ends together.
7. Whipstitch the shaped circle of material, where the ends were sewn together, onto the side of the head in the desired position.
8. Create and sew the second ear, of equal size, the same way.

NOTE: Use a double strand of all-purpose thread in the needle.

Perk up your monkey's ears!
Buttons, sparkle balls, earring letters, or jewelry make great monkey earlobe adornment!

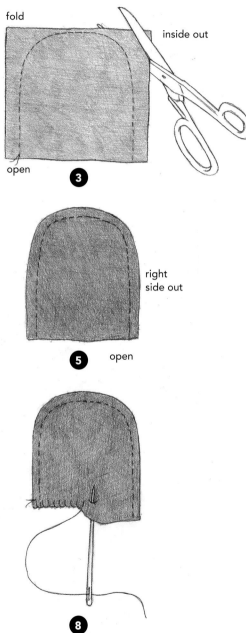

Formed Ears with an Outer Edge and the Inner Ear Stuffed

1. Fold one piece of the ear sock material inside out with right sides together.
2. Use a small running stitch, backstitch, or machine stitch to sew the folded material together with cream-colored thread to form the ear shape. Do not sew closed the side of the ear to be sewn to the monkey's head.
3. Trim the seam excess to within ¼ inch (6 mm) of the sewn ear shape.
4. Turn the sock material right side out.
5. Use a small running stitch or machine stitch to sew the outer circumference of the ear about ⅜ to ⅝ inch (1 to 1.5 cm) away from the outside edge of the ear. Do not sew closed the side of the ear to be sewn to the monkey's head.
6. Stuff the remaining space within the ear lightly with stuffing.
7. Fold in the raw edges at the open ear end.
8. Whipstitch the ear opening closed.
9. Whipstitch the ear onto the head in the desired position.
10. Create and sew the second ear, of equal size, the same way.

NOTE: *Use a double strand of all-purpose thread in the needle.*

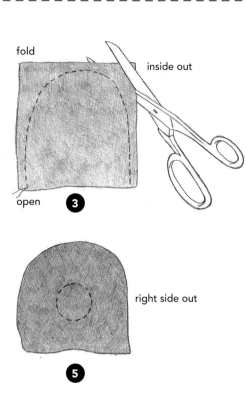

Formed Ears with an Inner Circle and the Outer Ear Stuffed

1. Fold one piece of the ear sock material inside out with right sides together.

2. Use a small running stitch, backstitch, or machine stitch to sew the folded material together with cream-colored thread to form the ear shape. Do not sew closed the side of the ear to be sewn to the monkey's head.

3. Trim the seam excess to within ¼ inch (6 mm) of the sewn ear shape.

4. Turn the sock material right side out.

5. Use a small running stitch or machine stitch to sew a small circle (about 1 inch [2.5 cm] in diameter) within the center of the ear. Do not sew closed the side of the ear to be sewn to the monkey's head.

6. Stuff the outer ear space lightly with stuffing.

7. Fold in the raw edges at the open ear end.

8. Whipstitch the ear opening closed.

9. Whipstitch the ear onto the head in the desired position.

10. Create and sew the second ear, of equal size, the same way.

NOTE: *Use a double strand of all-purpose thread in the needle.*

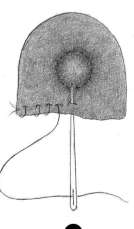

Out of This World Ears

1. Fold one piece of the ear sock material inside out with right sides together.

2. Use a small running stitch, backstitch, or machine stitch to sew the folded material together with cream-colored thread to form the ear shape. Do not sew closed the side of the ear to be sewn to the monkey's head.

3. Trim the seam excess to within ¼ inch (6 mm) of the sewn ear shape.

4. Turn the sock material right side out.

5. Stuff the ear lightly, leaving the shape flat in appearance, or do not stuff at all.

6. Fold in the raw edges at the open ear end.

7. Whipstitch the ear opening closed.

8. Whipstitch the ear onto the head in the desired position.

9. Create and sew the second ear, of equal size, the same way.

NOTE: *Use a double strand of all-purpose thread in the needle.*

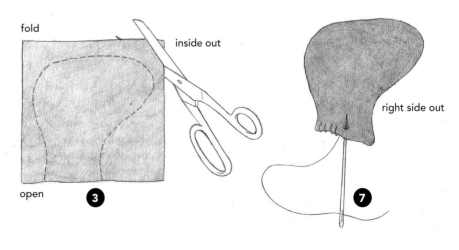

Rolled Ears

Most times, sock fabric from an extra red-heel sock is required to create rolled ears, but if you make your monkey's arms thin, you can create rolled ears without using a third sock. The key to rolled ears is having a thin length of fabric available to create the ears, for the longer the length of ear material, the larger the rolled ear will be!

1. Wrap and overlap ear material right side out around a pencil or long rod.
2. With cream-colored thread, whipstitch the length of material together along the pencil, tucking the raw edges under as each stitch is made.
3. Slip the pencil out from the material.
4. Fold in the raw edges at both ends.
5. Whipstitch the ends closed.
6. Roll the material into a circular shape, like a rolled garden hose.
7. Sew each evolving circle to the preceding circle with several small, well-placed whipstitches along each circle to hold one roll to the next, hiding your stitches, until the entire ear is sewn together. Whichever side of the ear you place your stitches on will be the back of the ear to hide the areas where stiches may be noticeable.
8. With the front side of the ear facing you, whipstitch a portion of the ear where the end of the last roll was completed onto the side of the head in the desired position.
9. Create and sew the second ear, of equal size, the same way.

NOTE: *Use a double strand of all-purpose thread in the needle.*

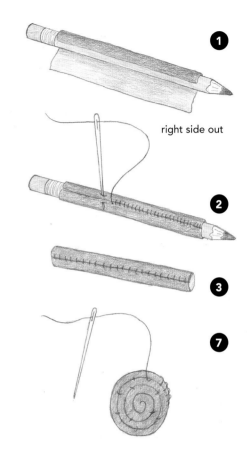

1

right side out

2

3

7

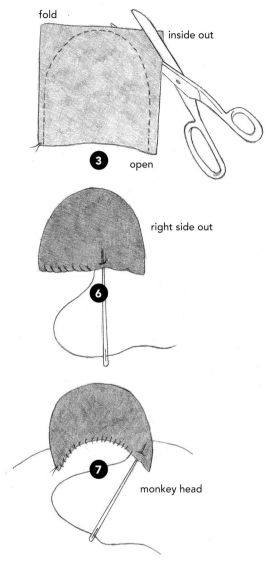

fold

inside out

open

3

right side out

6

7

monkey head

Cupped Ears

1. Fold one piece of the ear sock material inside out with right sides together.

2. Use a small running stitch, backstitch, or machine stitch to sew the folded material together with cream-colored thread to form the ear shape. Do not sew closed the side of the ear to be sewn to the monkey's head.

3. Trim the seam excess to within ¼ inch (6 mm) of the sewn ear shape.

4. Turn the sock material right side out.

5. Stuff the ear lightly. Fold in the raw edges at the open ear end.

6. Whipstitch the ear opening closed.

7. Whipstitch the ear onto the head in the desired placement, but change the direction of the ear in the middle of the seam to give the ear a "cupped" (crescent moon shape) appearance.

8. Create and sew the second ear, of equal size, the same way.

NOTE: *Use a double strand of all-purpose thread in the needle.*

Don't take a browbeating! If you do not want to pluck out unwanted eyebrow stitches on your sock monkey, be sure to put your monkey's brows to the test on paper first. Another way to easily experiment is to take a piece of loose, dark-colored yarn or felt material and cut it into different eyebrow lengths. Then place the loose yarn pieces at different distances above the eyes and contour them into different eyebrow shapes. Trust your instincts to determine what looks good on your monkey. You will be surprised at the many different looks your sock monkey can express—comical, primal, or something in between—without raising an eyebrow!

Eyebrows can be easily added with paint, markers, or embroidery thread. Faux fur, foam sheet, felt, or other materials can also be whipstitched on with all-purpose thread or glued onto your monkey. Embroidered eyebrows are typically sewn on with backstitches and are usually added before the main body is stuffed. Eyebrows applied with paint, marker, or glue are normally added after the main body is stuffed.

EYEBROWS

Eyebrows are not overlooked in our own grooming and they should not be overlooked in the creation of your sock monkey. Although they are not a necessary characteristic of your monkey, they can be a primary facial feature and play a dominant role in establishing facial expression. Different eyebrows can suggest a variety of moods and are worth exploring because they help convey the persona of your monkey. See page 164 for fun design inspiration.

Common eyebrow styles are typically rounded, angled, curved, or flat, and eyebrow thickness, length, and placement can quickly alter your sock monkey's overall expression. Eyebrows can be created in one smooth sweep, in dashes, or even as one long unibrow.

Tip
Crafters or caregivers who are fond of eyebrow piercing can add eyebrow rings for bling!

FALSE EYELASHES AND EYE SHADOW
Eyelashes

Early sock monkey pioneer crafters typically embroidered eyelashes onto their monkeys in simple or fanciful ways that continue to look great on any generation of sock monkey. But a new wave of artisans, using inexpensive products in the marketplace, are giving sock monkeys' peepers a whole new distinctive look with lifelike false lashes from the doll craft aisle or cosmetic line.

Doll eyelashes are available in several different sizes and can be cut to the desired size both in length and in depth. Every other eyelash can be snipped off short to give yet another look. There are usually a number of lengths of eyelashes in a pack of false doll eyelashes, so experiment!

Cosmetic false eyelashes come primarily sized to our own eyes, but like doll lashes, these can be cut to accent your monkey's eyes, too.

Artificial eyelashes are best added before the monkey's eyes are applied, or it will be difficult to sew the eyelash strands onto the monkey without space showing between the eyelashes and the top of each eye, should a seamless appearance be desired.

Eyelashes are added after the main body is stuffed.

Artificial lashes like this bride's doll lashes or cosmetic false eyelashes are such a wow feature you may not want to add eyebrows to keep the focus on the eyes!

Don't be in a rush to sew on artificial eyelashes! They are delicate. Care needs to be taken to obtain good results.

If you want your monkey's eyelashes to have a contour like our own natural lashes, cut the lashes to the length and depth needed for your monkey, and contour them similarly.

Artificial eyelashes are easily sewn as "sleepers," because there is no eye composition to contour. Another easy way to apply eyelashes is to pair them with felt eyes. Apply the felt eyes with glue to abut against the lashes after the eyelashes are sewn on.

If there are sock fabric nubs showing between the eyelashes and the eyes, redo either the eyelashes or the eyes, or take a similarly colored marker and dab over the sock nubs so they are not as noticeable.

How to Attach False Lashes

1. Loosely place your sock monkey's eyes in the desired position on your monkey's face.

2. Closely trace a portion of the upper arc of each eye onto the sock fabric with a pencil, and then remove the eyes. (These arcs will be a guide to place and sew the artificial strand of eyelashes.)

3. Gently fan out an eyelash strand to contour one of the arcs.

4. Trim the lash strand to the desired arc length.

5. Count the number of individual lashes in the desired length and cut another strand the same length.

6. Trim both eyelash strands to the desired depth and contour.

7. Snip every other lash to a shorter lash length or completely remove every other lash (optional).

8. Set one of the two eyelash strands aside.

9. Sew one stitch, matching thread color to the eyelash strand, into the fabric at the end of the pencil arc.

10. Push the thread knot end under the sock fabric surface to hide the knot.

11. Place the end of the eyelash strand over the stitch made on the pencil arc and whipstitch the end of the eyelash strand in place with all-purpose thread, overlapping stitches several times in the same position to anchor the lash strand.

12. Sew the entire strand of lashes to the sock fabric using a whipstitch between each lash to secure the lash strand to the fabric, taking care to sew the lash strand so the strand covers the pencil arc.

13. Sew several overlapping whipstitches at the end of the lash strand, knot, tie off, and hide the end knot below the surface of the sock fabric.

14. Sew the second eyelash strand, of equal size and contour, the same way on the other pencil arc.

Eye Shadow

Sock monkey eyes can be more impressive and expressive when accented with eye shadows of various colors, especially to emphasize femininity, masculinity, eeriness, or other characteristics.

First, practice the techniques below on comparable material to achieve eye-startling results, and then apply this technique to your monkey.

Eye shadow is typically applied after the main body is stuffed and after the eyes, eyelashes, eyebrows, and other facial features are added to the monkey.

• Shadow the area around each eye of your monkey with a permanent nontoxic flat-edged marker. Lightly press the marker edge onto the sock fabric surrounding one of your monkey's eyes in a sweeping motion, and then repeat the technique on the other eye. Go back and forth to each eye, shading the eyes similarly, until the shadow darkness and space covered is to your liking. Black or brown markers are neutral colors to use for any sock monkey persona, and often essential colors for eyes of spooky characters that come out at night!

• Shadow the area around each eye of your monkey with real eye shadow. Lightly press the brush onto the sock fabric surrounding one of your monkey's eyes in a sweeping motion, and then repeat the technique on the other eye. Go back and forth to each eye, shading the eyes similarly to your liking. Try colorful eye shadow with sparkle to add glimmer if you want a monkey's girly-girl image to stand out!

FINGERS, TOES, NAILS, WRISTS, AND ANKLES

When something extra special is needed to further exemplify your monkey's persona, give your monkey defined finger and toe digits, colorful nails, and wrists or ankles to parody simian or humanlike hands and feet. These features speak highly of a crafter who goes all out, for they take time! Liken this effort to running a race, crossing the finish line, and then running another mile! The result is well worth the effort and will make your monkey extraordinary!

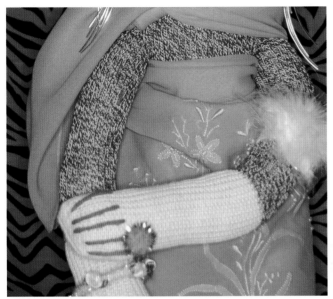

Crafters can effortlessly simulate temporary digits and nails like Zha-Zha's and Suzie's or permanent digits and nails.

SURFACE DIGITS AND NAILS

Fingers and toes can be embroidered, colored, or painted with any color, but brown and black typically look best for male-oriented monkeys. If you want to play manicurist, give your monkey a beauty treatment—embroider shorter lengths to emulate nails. The only tough question is whether to make either of these exemplary features temporary or permanent.

Fingers and toes and nails are applied after the sock monkey is created.

Change nonpermanent digits and nails periodically to reflect the color of your monkey's mood and dress.

The lengths of nails are typically shorter than fingers and toes.

The key to making distinct digits and nails is to first practice on an extra piece of sock fabric or similar material before you add the features to your monkey. An easy way to help you assess the length and placement of digits or nails is to place various lengths of embroidery thread on the ends of your sock monkey's limbs until you find what looks good.

Temporary Digits or Nails Created with a Continuous Length of Thread

***NOTE:** This technique works well when all digits are the same color.*

1. Draw lightly with a pencil five lengths of equally spaced digits or nails onto the sock surface of your monkey's limbs, as close to the end of each limb seam as possible.

2. Insert the threaded needle through the top of the sock surface next to your first pencil mark as close to the end seam of the limb as possible (but not directly in the stitch work of the end seam), and bring the needle up at the beginning of the first pencil mark. (This will be the start point to create your first length of a digit or nail.)

3. Insert the needle into the sock fabric at the end of the pencil mark, letting the thread lay smooth, but not loose, over the surface, with the needle coming up at the beginning of the second mark. Repeat this process until all five digits or nails are completed.

4. Knot and cut the thread. Push the knots below the surface of the sock.

5. Repeat this process with one length of embroidery floss until all five digits or nails are completed in consecutive order on each limb.

Temporary Digits or Nails Created with Individual Lengths of Embroidery Thread

***NOTE:** This technique works well when each digit will be a different color.*

1. Draw lightly with a pencil five lengths of equally spaced digits or nails onto the sock surface of your monkey's limbs, as close to the end of each limb seam as possible.

2. Insert the threaded needle through the top of the sock surface next to the first pencil mark, considered the first digit, as close to the end seam of the limb as possible (but not directly in the stitch work of the end seam), and bring the needle up at the beginning of the first pencil mark.

3. Insert the needle into the fabric at the end of the pencil mark, letting the thread lay smooth, but not loose, over the surface with the needle coming up as close to the end of the digit as possible.

4. Knot and cut the thread. Push the knots below the surface of the sock.

5. Repeat this process until all five digits or nails are completed in consecutive order on each limb.

Permanent Digits or Nails

***NOTE:** This technique works well when each digit will be the same or a different color.*

1. Draw lightly with a pencil the lengths of equally spaced digits or nails onto the sock surface of your monkey's limbs, as close to the end of each limb seam as possible.

2. Color each digit or nail over the penciled marks with nontoxic, permanent, washable fabric paint, medium-line colored marker, or nail polish.

3. Set the monkey aside to dry as required.

SCULPTED DIGITS, WRISTS, AND ANKLES

Fingers, toes, and other features can be sculpted. When sculpted with a double strand of all-purpose cream-colored thread, this stitch work blends realistically into the cream-colored areas of the monkey's limbs. This rarely seen technique is representative of a highly skilled crafter who has raised the monkey bar. These exemplary features typically appraise high on the Monk-O-Meter!

Sculpture is added to a sock monkey's limbs after the sock monkey is created.

Fingers and Toes

1. Draw lightly with a pencil four lengths of equally spaced digits (to create five separtions) onto the sock surface of your monkey's limbs to the end of each limb seam.

2. Insert the needle from the underside of the sock monkey limb up through to the topside at the end of the first pencil mark of the finger or toe (the end away from the limb seam).

3. Push the entire needle through the limb.

4. Sew a whipstitch down and around the edge of the limb seam and back up through the limb to where you first pushed the needle tip up through the sock, making the first length of a finger or toe.

5. Sew overlapping whipstitches several times in this same spot, pulling the thread tight to indent the sock fabric the length of the digit pencil mark to shape a distinct finger or toe.

6. Knot and cut the thread.

7. Push the knots of each digit below the surface.

8. Repeat this process until all digits are completed in consecutive order on each limb, creating the look of five digits.

Hands, top

Colorful nails are best applied after sculpting wrists and ankles, when the length of the hand and foot is known.

Wrists

1. Draw lightly with a pencil a line around the sock monkey's arm where you want to shape a wrist.
2. Thread the needle with a double strand of all-purpose cream-colored thread. Wrap the thread continuously around this penciled line several times, overlapping the threads and pulling the thread tight with each round to make an indentation emulating a wrist.
3. Knot and cut the thread.
4. Push the knot below the surface of the sock.
5. Repeat this process for the other wrist at a matching location.

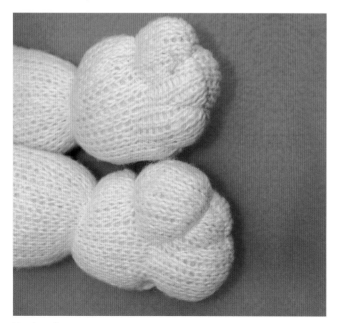

Hands, palm

Foot, top

Ankles

1. Draw lightly with a pencil a line around the sock monkey leg where you want to shape the bend of the limb to emulate an ankle.

2. Thread the needle with a double strand of all-purpose cream-colored thread. Wrap the thread continuously around this penciled line several times, overlapping the threads and pulling the thread tight with each round to make an indentation emulating an ankle.

3. Knot and cut the thread.

4. Push the knot below the surface of the sock.

5. Bend the end of the leg limb, where you pulled the thread tight, toward the front of the leg to emulate an ankle bend.

6. Sew the bend together with small whipstitches to lock the ankle bend in place, pulling the thread tight with each stitch, to pull the fabric at the bend together for a seamless look.

7. Sew the bend together again to reinforce the stitch work.

8. Knot and cut the thread.

9. Push the knots below the surface of the sock.

10. Repeat this process for the other ankle at a matching location.

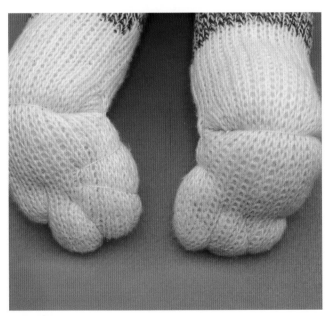

Foot, sole

HAIR

Hair can serve as the pièce de résistance to your sock monkey's appearance! While bald is beautiful on any sock monkey, hair of any kind or amount on your monkey's chrome dome can pull together the total image you want your monkey to project. Hair adds such an "awww" factor that even a bad hair day looks adorable on a sock monkey.

There are many quality hairlike materials available in different colors to adorn your monkey's crown, including faux fur, hair pieces, doll hair, doll wigs, fleece, fringe trim, garland, felt, or yarn. Snippets of colorful boas or bright neon hair scrunchies can add instant humor to a monkey, especially if you are making a monkey roadie, a monkey fit for *tails from the Crypt,* or an action hero superstar.

Bangs, ponytails, braids, mohawks, crew cuts—anything goes! Add a full crown of hair or a swatch of hair—whatever turns you and your monkey on! Can't decide on one? Don't! Change your monkey's hair just like we do for a special occasion or when your sock monkey mojo prompts a different style or cut. And then twist it, bead it, braid it, spike it, curl it, or kink it!

Your sock monkey is ready for its hairdo after the main body is stuffed and the facial features, ears, arms, and tail have been added. Hair is typically whipstitched on using all-purpose thread or glued onto your monkey's head before you add a sock cap or other head topper.

As monkeys progress **higher on the Monk-O-Meter Money Scale, they typically have hair. Doll wigs, faux hair, felt, yarn, or colorful trim is often added onto the monkey's pate in a color similar to the recipient's hair color. If you do not find materials to make a fabulous head of hair for your monkey in the craft and fabric aisles, another option is to purchase a stuffed animal and use its faux fur.**

Use a needle for heavier-weight material to sew on a thick hair piece. A finger thimble will help push the needle through the hair and sock fabric, lessen resistance, and save your sewing finger from soreness.

Doll Wig

1. Measure the circumference of your monkey's crown to identify the approximate doll wig size to buy.

2. Place the wig on your monkey's head to identify the best placement.

3. Use matching thread to sew the wig around the entire circumference of your monkey's head, with small whipstitches, pulling all stitches tight as you sew without breaking the thread. (Tightening the thread as you sew will help hide the thread within the hairline for a more seamless, natural look.)

4. With your needle, flick free the ends of any hair strands that may have gotten caught in your whip-stitches at the hairline. This cleanup step is often unavoidable if you sew, rather than glue, a wig onto your monkey.

5. Push the knots below the surface of the sock.

Doll wigs with a circumference of 8 to 10 inches (20.3 to 25.5 cm) will typically fit the head of a standard-size sock monkey created from size large red-heel socks. Measure the circumference of your monkey's crown to identify the exact wig size.

Swatch of Faux Fur

1. Cut a swatch of faux fur, cutting through the fabric of the faux fur only, not the strands of faux fur, in the size desired.

2. Sew small whipstitches, with thread to match the color of the faux fur swatch, to secure the entire swatch onto the crown of your monkey's head, pulling all stitches tight as you sew without breaking the thread. (Tightening the thread as you sew will help hide the thread within the hairline for a more seamless, natural look.)

3. With your needle, flick free the ends of hair strands that may have gotten caught in your whipstitches at the hairline. This cleanup step is often unavoidable if you sew, rather than glue, the swatch onto your monkey.

4. Push the knots below the surface of the sock.

Full Head of Faux Fur Hair

1. Place a piece of faux fur material over your monkey's crown, wrong side facing up.

2. Draw lightly with a pencil a rough circular shape on the wrong side of the faux fur material in the largest size you would want your monkey's head of hair to be.

3. Remove the material from your monkey's head.

4. With the scissors tips, cut through the fabric of the faux fur only, not the strands of faux fur, along the penciled circle.

5. Place the cut hair piece onto your monkey's crown for an exact "fitting."

6. Trim the hair piece to the desired size as needed.

7. With thread matching the color of the faux fur hair piece, sew a few small whipstitches to anchor the hair piece to the crown of your monkey's head, beginning at the hairline above the left ear as the monkey faces you.

8. Cup the hair piece around your monkey's head with your hand to gauge whether the hair piece can be sewn onto the head with the material lying smoothly without puckers. If there are no material puckers, skip the next four steps.

9. Stuff the area between the head and hair with fiberfill to help create a smooth contoured look, eliminating material pucker. (If fiberfill eliminates material pucker, then skip the next three steps. If fiberfill does not eliminate material pucker, the next two steps are key in giving your monkey a smooth head of hair.)

10. Gauge how many folds of material may need to be made for the hair piece to lie smoothly on your monkey's head by overlapping the hair piece at equal distances on each side of the center back to equally release the tension of hair bumps. Sometimes the folding of hair, depending on the material used, may cause thick overlaps of hair along the hairline, making any contour folding of material visually noticeable. If this occurs, then slit the folds with scissors. (You will know which method you should use—fold or snip a slit—once you overlap the fabric ¼ to ½ inch [6 to 13 mm] and see how thick the bump of the fold is. If too thick, cut a slit at the fold line and overlap the cut edges of the slit material to keep the hair piece lying as flat as possible on your monkey's head.)

11. Sew small whipstitches to secure each folded overlap, or the overlapped edges of slit folds, along the edge of the faux hair piece.

12. Sew small whipstitches to secure the fitted hair piece onto the crown of your monkey's head, moving from the left ear over to the front forehead, over to your monkey's right ear, and around the back of the hair piece until you meet up to your starting position at the left ear. Pull all stitches tight as you sew without breaking the thread. (Tightening the thread as you sew will help hide the thread within the hairline for a more seamless, natural look.)

13. With your needle, flick free the ends of any hair strands that may have gotten caught in your whipstitches at the hairline. This cleanup step is often unavoidable if you sew, rather than glue, the hair piece onto your monkey.

14. Push the knots below the surface of the sock.

The same material used for a monkey's moustache and beard is also typically used for the monkey's eyebrows. The use of like material adds continuity to a monkey's look and avoids visually hairy "speed bumps" unless desired.

MOUSTACHES AND BEARDS

Very few sock monkeys have moustaches or beards. Perhaps crafters forgo this feature because it is the hairiest facial feature to apply and obtain an aesthetically pleasing look. But if you are creating a spoofy character who is a refined bon vivant, or personalizing a sock monkey for a loved one or friend who has a moustache, beard, or both, it is essential for you to know how to apply these features.

Common shapes of moustaches, based on character traits attributed to societal stereotypes, are highlighted in the Moustaches illustration on page 164 to help you personalize your sock monkey into a movie star, villain, hero, rock star, friend, classmate, or *sole* mate.

Most moustaches and beards (or goatees) look best on monkeys when they match the head of hair with like materials and colors, but unexpected delights await those who dare to mix and match colors and textures in this "hair-raising" experience!

A moustache or beard is typically attached after the sock monkey is completed.

Tip
A smidge of oil like olive or baby oil will go a long way in keeping flyaway hair groomed. Place a small drop or two of oil on your fingers, rub your fingers together to dissipate the drops, and then smooth the oil with your fingertips onto unruly hair, moustaches, or beards.

Moustaches

Handmade moustaches are typically created from faux fur or other imitation hairlike materials with some surface texture. They can also be created from felt or foam sheet, but they may not appear as realistic. Check out the mustache designs on page 164. Ready-made costume moustaches can be purchased as a viable option, too. They tend to give a sock monkey an exaggerated look.

Depending on the material used, sew small whipstitches to secure the moustache onto your monkey's mouth piece using all-purpose thread to match the color of the moustache, or use glue to affix the piece. Flick free the ends of any hair strands that may have gotten caught in your whipstitches. This cleanup step is often unavoidable if you sew, rather than glue, a moustache onto your monkey. Push the knots below the surface of the sock.

Sometimes the entire moustache does not need to be fully sewn or glued. If the ends of the moustache extend beyond the monkey's cheeks, only the portion that lies against the sock fabric is anchored.

Experiment first! Trace and cut moustaches out of paper similar to ones found in the Moustaches illustration on page 165, and try them on your monkey for size. Adjust length and width accordingly, as each monkey's mug is different!

Beards

When you want your monkey to make a statement, make it loud and clear! A beard lends credence to certain sock monkey personas, and when one is missing, the characterization is simply lost. Chin hair is typically created from faux fur, boa snippets, yarn, or fanciful trim. If you want to braid and bead your monkey's beard, be sure to choose beard material that will separate into strands long enough to braid.

Most times, only the upper edge of the beard is sewn or glued onto the monkey below the red-heel area of the monkey's mouth piece, for any material extending past the chin no longer has an anchor point.

If you don't want to go through the fuss of sewing or gluing a permanent beard onto your monkey's chin, and the recipient of your monkey is four years of age or older, tie a string onto each side of the beard and tie the beard strings together behind your monkey's head like Lil Abe's. No one will think less of you—honest!

Usually, the same faux fur material can be used for moustaches, beards, eyebrows, hair, and even ear hair, if desired! This Santa is all set to spread holiday cheer. Ho! Ho! Ho!

Faux Fur Moustache or Beard

1. Cut a swatch of faux fur, cutting through the base fabric only, not the strands of faux fur, in the moustache or beard shape desired.

2. Place the moustache or beard in the desired position.

3. Sew small whipstitches to secure the moustache or beard in place, with all-purpose thread to match the swatch of faux fur, pulling all stitches tight as you sew without breaking the thread. (Tightening the thread as you sew will help hide the thread within the moustache or beard hairline for a more seamless, natural look.)

4. Flick free the ends of any hair strands that may have gotten caught in your whipstitches. This cleanup step is often unavoidable if you sew, rather than glue, facial hair onto your monkey.

5. Push the knots below the surface of the sock.

MOUTH SHAPES

Today's crafters who are on the cutting edge of designing cute and collectible sock monkeys that will climb high on the Monk-O-Meter Money Scale dare to be different in all facets of monkey making. These crafters give their monkeys irresistible, distinctive mouth shapes by reshaping the red-heel mouth piece in various ways. Six techniques for enhancing your monkey's most flamboyant attribute—its colorful red-heel mouth (or lips)—are outlined here. Whether your ideal monkey is in need of upturned, kissable, pursed, or other lips, quick solutions are at your fingertips, with plenty left for you to explore on your own.

If cream-colored nubs peek through your embroidered areas when you are finished, don't worry! Either redo your stitch work or take a red marker, similar in color to the embroidered thread, and dab the unsightly nubs red.

Lips can also be outlined with backstitches like Ernie's pal, Sally, who also has a Kissy Face technique applied, as on page 104.

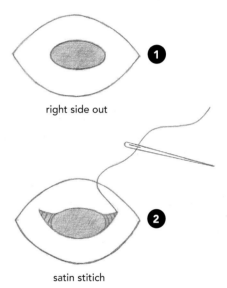

right side out

1

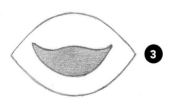

satin stitich

2

3

Mouth Upswing

Add an "upswing" to your modern monkey's red-heel mouth with only a few well-placed stitches! Love-struck Ernie has the upper corners of his red-heel mouth piece satin stitched, simulating the natural knitted smile of a vintage sock monkey.

For a smile like Ernie's, satin stitch both upper corners of the elongated red oval of the mouth piece with red embroidery thread to match the color of the red heel. Hide your knots below the sock surface.

Apply this technique after the red-heel mouth piece is sewn onto your monkey, taking care not to pucker the lips with stitch work that is too tight. The technique can also be applied before the red mouth is sewn on. In this way, all knots can be made below the surface of the sock. You decide!

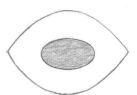

right side out

Kissy Face

Do you prefer the look of curvaceous lips like this vintage sun worshipper? You'll be pleased to know that you can easily create a "kissy face" look on vintage or modern red-heel monkeys.

Apply this technique after the red-heel mouth piece is sewn onto your monkey.

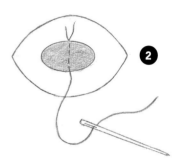

1. Sew two small, overlapping stitches with matching red thread to anchor the thread at the middle of the top edge of the red-heel mouth piece.

2. Sew very small running stitches going downward vertically until you reach the bottom edge of the red heel. Do not tie off and cut the thread yet.

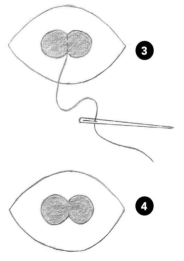

3. Pull the thread at the bottom edge of the red heel until the center top fabric of the red heel moves toward the bottom of the red heel to achieve the "kissy" shape desired.

4. Knot and cut the thread.

5. Push the knots below the surface of the sock.

NOTES: *Use a double strand of all-purpose thread in the needle.*

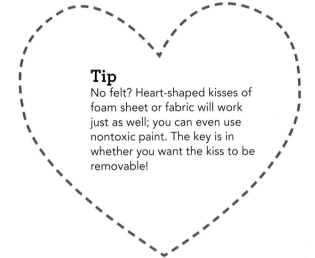

HeartFELT Kisses

Are you looking for the simplest way to add kissable lips to your monkey? Cut a small heart from whatever color of felt material you prefer. Center the heart in your monkey's red-heel mouth piece and glue the heart onto your monkey for an instant, seamless pucker like Mattie's! Or sew the heart on with a few stitches to make it removable.

Apply either technique after the red-heel mouth piece is stuffed and sewn onto your monkey.

1. Cut a heart in the shape desired.

2. Center the heart on your monkey's red-heel mouth piece.

3. Glue or sew small whipstitches to secure the heart in place with thread to match the heart, pulling all stitches tight as you sew without breaking the thread. (Tightening the thread as you sew will help hide the thread within both fabrics for a more seamless, natural kiss.)

4. Push the knots below the surface of the sock.

NOTE: *Use a double strand of all-purpose thread in the needle.*

Tip
No felt? Heart-shaped kisses of foam sheet or fabric will work just as well; you can even use nontoxic paint. The key is in whether you want the kiss to be removable!

Mum's the word! Miss Frumpy's lips are sealed tighter than tight. You are not getting any sass out of her!

Miss Monet has it and loves to flaunt it! The cream color and red heel of her mouth piece have both been contoured and the Kissy Face technique applied as well.

Frumpy, Perky, or Quirky Mouth

Would you like your monkey to have thin or uneven lips like Miss Frumpy's? Or would you prefer your *sole* mate have a smaller mouth to reflect perky, pouty, or dainty charm like Miss Monet? Whatever you decide, a funky, quirky mouth for your vintage or modern sock monkey is easily created by changing the shape of the red heel, the cream-colored area of the red-heel mouth piece, or both.

Apply this technique after the red-heel mouth piece is stuffed and sewn onto your monkey (see illustrations on page 107).

1. Fold and squish together the red-heel area of the mouth piece or the cream-colored area with your fingers. Cover up as much or as little of the area until you have the size and shape you desire.

2. Hold the shape with one hand, and with the other hand, whipstitch this newly shaped contour in place with matching thread, pulling all the stitches tight as you sew. (Tightening the thread as you sew will help hide the thread within the sock fabric for a more seamless, natural look.)

3. Push the knots below the surface of the sock.

4. Embellish further with other techniques, if desired.

NOTES: *Use a double strand of all-purpose thread in the needle.*

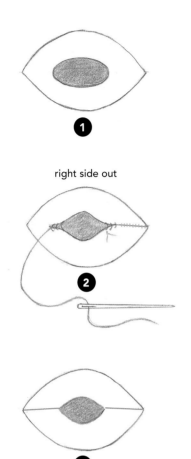

right side out

Topsy-Turvy

Your vintage sock monkey's personality can radiate with a "right-side up" or an "upside down" red-heel mouth piece. Before you add a smile line to your red-heel mouth piece, and before you whipstitch the mouth piece onto your monkey, turn the entire mouth piece topsy-turvy to make the red smile edges swing up or swing down. The choice is yours!

Unwanted knitted cream-colored thread might show within the colorful red-heel mouth area of the sock, taking away from your sock monkey's persona. A crafty crafter can use a matching red, fine-point, nontoxic permanent marker to skim over the cream thread to remove such blemishes, if desired.

Seeking another look? Before you sew on the mouth piece, fold most of the cream color of the mouth piece under, shaping the mouth piece similar to Spud's. Only most of the flashy red heel shows, giving Spud an impish appearance!

The rosy cheeks of the bonny lass, Ava, were dabbed on with rouge using a fingertip.

ROSY CHEEKS

Sock monkeys with cheeks all aglow are extra special. Rosy cheeks add to childlike wonder, from a blushing beauty queen or granny to the "Ho-Ho-Ho" of Santa Claus or a monkey dancing a jig!

There are a number of materials available to create monkey glow. Put the "rosy" in your monkey's cheeks with rouge powder, smudged lipstick, diluted food coloring, sparkle fabric paints, and more.

Experiment with different color hues of pinks and reds. Decide on whether you want to use your index finger or a brush to dab on color. Practice first with the product you want to use for this distinguished feature on similar fabric, as chances are they will leave some trace of discoloring if you make a mistake and try to remove them.

When you are ready to add this cheeky feature to your monkey, be sure to apply the color lightly within a small area and gradually increase the color and size of the area until you have the overall glow you want to achieve.

Glow should be applied to your sock monkey's cheeks after the mouth piece is stuffed and sewn onto your monkey.

One way to apply lipstick or rouge is to dab a little on your index finger and then rub your finger gently on paper to remove the initial thick residue from your fingertip. Then rub your fingertip onto a small area of one monkey cheek as the "hub" of darkest color, and rub the glow outward to affect a natural shading of color. Repeat this technique until you see the size of glow that looks best before moving on to the other cheek and repeating the process.

SHAPELY SECRETS

If you want to create a sophisticated sock monkey in the likeness of an action hero, an athletic competitor, or a sexy dude or diva known for bulging muscles or splendidly formed curves, add some muscle and contour! Body-shaping your sock monkey is a supreme example of the art of monkeying around, and you need not take your monkey to the gym to get its nubs into great shape.

The easiest ways to mold muscles for a *sockpendous* figure, without sweat equity, is to shape, cinch, or sew them. Sculpt a dramatic physique through the placement and

displacement of stuffing, cinch a limb to emulate a muscle or two, or sew a shapely physique. Almost any body part, such as the monkey head, neck, waistline, triceps, biceps, thighs, and calves, can become pronounced, sensational features with one or more of these techniques and make a lasting impression.

- **SCULPT.** Adjust amounts of stuffing used in specific areas of monkey parts and softly sculpt the parts with your hands to form shapeliness. This sculpting technique should be done while you stuff the main body and limbs of the monkey.

- **CINCH**. Wrap matching thread tightly around the body part to be emphasized, snuggly cinching the thread tight without breaking it, then tie off. Push the knot below the surface of the sock. This method works well to create instant muscle definition, bulges, and curves on sections of arms and legs. A monkey's waistline can also be cinched, but use a heavier thread than all-purpose thread because the area to cinch is expansive and will put light thread under stress. A cinch made with heavy thread will be covered when clothes are added. This sculpting technique is done after the main body of the monkey and limbs are stuffed. Try it—you'll like it, for it's a cinch!

- **SEW CURVES.** Sew curves into your sock monkey parts to accentuate shapely features. This sculpting technique is done while the seams of the sock parts are being sewn, with the parts turned inside out and not yet stuffed. The seams can be sewn with running stitches or backstitches, or machine sewn. Do not make any shapely areas on the main body or other parts too small or narrow for you to turn the sock part right side out after you finish.

Sockeye has eaten his spinach! He has a contoured head, thin neck, and muscles in the arms—all sculpted by machine. Would you like exaggerated muscles on your monkey? Sculpt, cinch, or sew curves!

TATTOOS

Tattoos are popular and can be a distinctive, fun way for crafters to personalize a sock monkey for themselves or someone who appreciates and admires this style of expressive art. Perhaps you or the intended recipient of your monkey are too timid to enter a tattoo parlor, but would love to live vicariously through a brave sock monkey!

Simple and stunning tattoo designs can be created by hand (see page 165 for ideas). A variety of tattoos are also available for purchase, such as this spoofy hatter's stick-on dragonfly. Most tattoos are applied after your sock monkey is completed.

- Design and embroider a tattoo onto your completed monkey.
- Paint a tattoo freehand, or with a stencil, onto your completed monkey with nontoxic, permanent, washable fabric paints.
- Create an appliqué tattoo from felt, foam sheets, or other materials and whipstitch or glue them onto your completed monkey.
- Apply appliqués or ready-made iron-on or sew-on patches, like Black Bart's, to your completed monkey.
- Buy ready-made foam shapes, jewelry, and gems and whipstitch or glue them onto your completed monkey.
- Buy removable gems and sticker shapes for a simple, nonpermanent tattoo solution and stick them onto your completed monkey.

Tip
Create a tattoo in different sizes to see what looks best on your monkey. Practice creating the tattoo on similar fabric first if the tattoo is to be applied with paint or other permanent material.

Explore favorite craft aisles for more tattoo ideas.

A simple red heart tattoo made from felt, like this sporty nubster, Lil' Pete's, can be sewn onto your monkey's chest, red-heel bum, or cheek as a universal winner.

TEETH/FANGS

Let's face it: while toothless grins are plentiful on sock monkeys, certain characters look false without their teeth showing. Can you imagine a blood-chilling vampire such as Count Sockula without fangs? Where teeth would be sorely missed, crafters can dabble in home dentistry to make their choppers come to life. No power drills or dentist chairs are necessary to give your monkey pearly whites!

Teeth attributes are applied after the sock monkey is completed.

- Design an outline of multiple teeth to fit your monkey's smile and embroider only the outline of multiple teeth with black embroidery thread onto the monkey's mouth piece with small running or backstitches. Push the knots below the sock surface.

- Design an outline of multiple teeth, like Count Socku-la's, to fit your monkey's smile. Embroider the outline with black embroidery thread onto the monkey's mouth piece with small running or backstitches. Push the knots under the sock surface. Satin stitch simulated teeth within the framework of the outline with white embroidery thread. Push the knots under the sock surface. If you do not sew a perfect row of teeth, remember you are sewing your ideal monkey, not a perfect monkey. Toothy grins, not always perfect, can be delightful when crooked!

Tip
Costume teeth or teeth that come in pumpkin creation kits are other toothsome sources to be considered!

Bitty Bite's fangs were cut from foam sheet and glued in place.

Rusty's outline of teeth was cut from foam sheet, and each individual tooth was outlined with a black marker. The border around the foam piece was then embroidered in black.

- Design an outline of multiple or individual teeth to fit your monkey's smile with black permanent marker, but practice the design on similar sock fabric before you permanently add teeth to your monkey's grin.

- Design an outline of multiple or individual teeth to fit your monkey's smile using products such as felt or foam sheet to make sock monkey choppers like Rusty's and Bitty Bites'. Cut desired material to fang, tooth, or grin size, and whipstitch or glue them onto your monkey.

The key to good sock monkey dentistry is to design various tooth outlines and individual teeth in different sizes and shapes. Loosely place the outlines or individual teeth of different sizes onto your monkey's red-heel mouth piece to decide which ones looks best. If your monkey has a smile line, the teeth should be placed against the underside of the smile line or within the smile lines after the sock monkey is completed.

TONGUES

Don't be tongue-tied! Adding a distinctive tongue feature to your sock monkey can lend a hint of humor, especially to mimic someone who is sick or being bratty! Felt tongues, whether made from a single layer of felt or a stuffed double layer, look swell on a sock monkey. Choose felt of different colors—even blue if your monkey is turning frigid from the cold, or green and spotted if feeling under the weather!

Experiment with various sizes and shapes of tongues by placing potential candidates on the red-mouth area. When monkeys have two smile lines that cover the entire width of the red-heel mouth area, tongues look best when placed between the smile lines. When they have one smile line, tongues are typically placed against the bottom or top of the smile line. When there is no smile line, anything goes! Let the sock monkey mojo within you decide which way is more tasteful for your monkey and maybe you'll come up with a whole new tantalizing look!

The top portion of the tongue can be glued or whip-stitched with all purpose thread onto the red-heel mouth piece. A sewn-on tongue won't have you tongue-tied like a glued one will, as a sewn tongue can be easily removed. But a sewn tongue can trip you up if you choose a tongue color other than a matching red, as the stitches may not easily blend and hide in the red-heel area. Tongues can also be made to loll or curl from a few small, well-placed whipstitches.

Tongues are applied after the sock monkey is completed.

All sock monkey moments are precious, but the unexpected ones are doubly so! One of my own memories fondly came to mind while I wrote this tantalizing section. I had placed a dampened sock monkey tongue in the freezer so the tongue would harden, taking on a specific shape for a "chef" photo shoot. Imagine my husband's reaction when he opened the freezer door. Talk about tongue-in-cheek!

"X" MARKS THE SPOT TO BOOTY UP!

A spot sorely missed for embellishment on most sock monkeys is their feet! If you don't want your monkey to be a tenderfoot and lose the race, there is an easy way to make it outrun the others! Simply take yarn or other lace-like materials and weave in some boots or shoes. With a quick flourish of your darning needle, your monkey will be laced up and ready to stomp around in ankle boots, walking boots, trooper boots, thigh-high boots—whatever height you determine is best. This mocked-up style of footwear will have your monkey walking tall within minutes. What color should the laces be? Coordinate lace colors to match or contrast with your monkey's pom-poms, eye color, or the clothes in its wardrobe, and change them out at whim.

Take a few minutes to explore the various ways to weave laces—intertwine colors and double or triple up on them like we sometimes do our own. There is no right or wrong way to lace. If you need a jump-start, the "X" Marks the Spot Design illustration (opposite) can help you begin.

Laces are added after your sock monkey is completed.

1. Cut a length of ribbon, yarn, or other lacelike materials to the desired length, or use real shoelaces as each simulated boot can typically be created with one shoelace and have length to spare.

2. Follow the illustrations on page 119 to weave the lace below and above the surface of the sock fabric to simulate the lacing of a real pair of boots. Use a darning needle that has an eye large enough to hold the thickness of the lace.

3. Shift the laces by hand if necessary so the ends are of equal size when completed.

4. Tie each lace end into a bow or wrap the lace ends around the leg and then tie.

5. Create the second laced boot, of equal size, the same way.

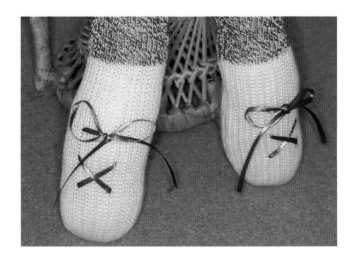

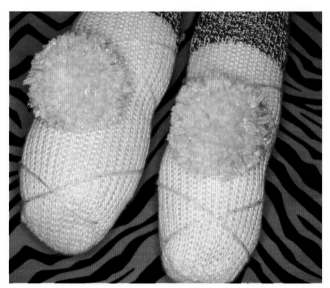

Makeshift laces, like these made with yarn, are so easy to create you will be exploring this distinctive feature on your own in no time!

If the Booty Up technique isn't quite right for your monkey's persona, consider using trim, colorful thread, or yarn around the cuff line of the legs, the tail, or even the arms.

"X" MARKS THE SPOT DESIGN

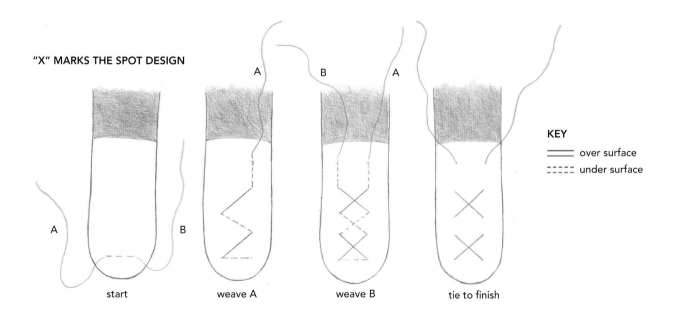

A   B

A   B   A

start   weave A   weave B   tie to finish

KEY

―――― over surface

------ under surface

Creating Your Ideal Sock Monkey

Monkey Madness Begins—Decision Time!

You now know how to design a unique, one-of-a-kind sock monkey pal and have hopefully "cottoned" to several *socky* techniques described herein. Maybe you have been inspired to try some of your own techniques to bring your monkey to life from the recesses and folds of your socks!

Now is the time for monkeyshines. Be knit picky and sketch your ideas before monkey making!

Before you begin to sew, regardless of whether you are a newbie or a seasoned crafter, you should first have a sense of what your sock monkey's persona will be. Included is a sock-monkey-friendly checklist to help you remember important attributes from chapters that may have charmed your socks off. Your answers will help you focus on basic and distinctive characteristics and features, one monkey at a time, and aid you in sketching your monkey.

Gather any *sockadoodle* notes scribbled thus far, review the text and matrices of the preceding chapters, and flip through the showcase of monkeys in these pages for inspiration. Then read through the Sock Monkey Pal Checklist on pages 122 to 123. Be sure to answer all questions, as they will help you eliminate monkey-making mayhem and bring together the features and attributes desired to make your cute and collectible sock monkey.

Know what you want your monkey to look like to avoid monkey meltdown during the creation process. In the very least, you should be able to relay invaluable, detailed information to someone else whom you may choose to create your ideal monkey for you, if you choose to take the monkey off your back!

Remember—don't forget to think about a nose!

SOCK MONKEY PAL CHECKLIST

1. Who will be the recipient of your monkey?

2. How old is this intended caregiver?

3. Do you have safety in mind? Sock monkey enthusiasts are encouraged to purchase other appropriate sock monkey novelty items suitable for children under the age of four. In this way, they can be introduced to the sock monkey tradition safely and be ready for their monkey when they are of the proper age!

4. What is the hair color, hairstyle, and eye color of the intended caregiver or character you want your monkey to spoof?

5. Does the intended caregiver or spoofy character wear glasses or have any endearing blemishes you might want to copy on your monkey?

6. What is the gender and physique of the intended caregiver or spoofy character you want your monkey to emulate?

7. What are the interests (from hobbies to favorite colors) of the intended caregiver or spoofy character (e.g., famous people, an occupation, military, sports figures, or others)? Indicate such features as colors of pom-poms, specific clothes, and accessories.

8. Based upon your answers to the above questions, decide on a general persona or theme for your sock monkey.

CAUTION: For safety reasons, it is not recommended that sock monkeys be created for children under the age of four or pets because small parts could cause a choking hazard. If the intended recipient of your sock monkey is under the age of four or a pet, do not proceed to create a monkey.

9. What style of red-heel socks do you want to use to make this creation: vintage, modern, or other?

10. What size socks do you prefer to use to make this creation? Will a certain sock size emphasize the physique of the caregiver or spoofy character? Adult S/M/L/XL, kid's small, miniature, or mixed sizes?

11. What *basic* characteristics and features do you want your sock monkey to possess in support of it's persona or theme? What techniques do you prefer to use to create them? Make specific notes for each attribute below:

    • Eyes and eyelashes

    • Smile line

    • Nose

    • Ears

    • Neckline

    • Body and limbs

    • Tail

    • Cap

    • Pom-poms

Inspiration for monkey monikers:

Have fun and choose a moniker for your monkey! Dinky, Stinkpot, Shufflebean, Wigglesquirt, Buzz, Finkus Stinkus, Kiki, Darling Darlyne, Ticklebean, Picklebean, Bitty Bites, Squidgy Widgy, Mitzie, Stumpy, Zippy, Spike, Dipsy Doodle, Squeaky, Lu-Lu, Pepito, Rusty, Big Joe—the funnier the merrier in the world of *sockmonkeydom!*

12. What *distinctive* characteristics and features do you want your sock monkey to possess in support of it's persona or theme? What techniques do you prefer to use to create them? Make specific notes for each attribute below:

    • Beauty marks (e.g., freckles and moles)

    • Belly button

    • Ears, ears, and more ears

    • Eyebrows

    • False eyelashes and eye shadow

    • Fingers, toes, and nails

    • Hair

    • Moustache/beard

    • Mouth shape

    • Rosy cheeks

    • Shapely secrets

    • Tattoos

    • Teeth/fangs

    • Tongue

    • "X" Marks the Spot to Booty Up

13. Do you want this monkey to endure lots of hugs? If so, amount of stuffing, double-sewn seams, and clothing styles may come into consideration.

14. What will be your monkey's moniker while you sew?

15. If the Monk-O-Meter Money Scale is important to you, do the basic and/or distinctive features you have selected meet monetary values you have set for your cute and collectible sock monkey? Remember, the Monk-O-Meter Money Scale is only a guide and is subject to the whims of the market.

SOCK MONKEY DESIGN WORKSHEET

By now you have a very good idea about how your new cute and collectible sock monkey will look based on information you gathered in the preceding chapters. Before you make the first stitch, let the creative artist within you burst out on paper! Socks are quite forgiving, and can handle most rework, but it will save you time and monkey meltdown if you sketch your monkey's image beforehand. Draw various looks for your sock monkey until you have your ideal monkey. Experiment with different sizes and placement of features and characteristics you identified on the Sock Monkey Pal Checklist, keeping safety in mind as you design.

Do not be in a hurry to create your pal! Monkey around, and if you do not like what you have drafted, go back to the drawing board and sketch some more. You have the creative power to alter your design until you discover one that emulates your imagined monkey-to-be. If you are supervising someone, or are sharing in the creation of a sock monkey with another person, use this time to get all your ideas on paper.

When you have a final sketch of your sock monkey, acquire all of the materials and supplies needed. Once you have your monkey makings, your monkey will soon be kicking up its heels, and so will you!

Be sure to give your monkey a recognizable monkey face in the spirit of tradition—unless, of course, your monkey is not of this world!

Look familiar? **This** *sockadoodle* **outline of Missy, who stars in this chapter, was first sketched in pencil and completed with colored pencils and markers per the basic and distinctive features identified in making notes from the Sock Monkey Pal Checklist on pages 122 to 123. Missy was machine sewn, with small parts hand sewn, and her persona embellished accordingly.**

SOCK MONKEY DESIGN WORKSHEET SAMPLE

Missy

SAMPLE NOTES FROM SOCK MONKEY PAL CHECKLIST

THEME: Female red-heel sock monkey with overall universal appeal, name of Missy:

- For my own collection
- Modern red-heel socks, one pair, size Large
- Basic double set of flat two-hole buttons—a small blue on top of a white—doubled together and sewn with black embroidery thread
- Basic five embroidered black eyelashes per eye, seamless look, six-ply strand
- Basic embroidered black nose, six-ply strand
- Basic embroidered solid black smile line extended outside of red-heel area, six-ply strand
- Basic body stuffed firm, but bendable
- Basic neck, red yarn necktie to make neck smaller to fit dress neck enclosure
- Basic tail—stuffed to be flexible to curl and uncurl
- Basic removable sock cap
- Distinctive ears with an outer edge and inner ear stuffed
- Distinctive blonde synthetic wiglet sewn to head
- Basic pom-poms, five yellow pom-poms attached with darning needle to arms, legs, and tail
- Handmade dress, doll shoes and socks, yellow hair bow

Monk-O-Meter Money Scale: **MEDIUM**

Sewing Your Sock Monkey

Let the sock monkey sewing jubilee begin! A swashbuckling pirate, beautiful princess, "rain-or-shine" postman, patriotic soldier, bad-to-the-nubs villain, wild and crazy football fan, sweet and sassy red-hatter, lazy beach bum—whatever sock monkey friend you designed in chapter 13 is waiting to leap from within the folds of your red-heel socks! You are now ready to monkey around. So get your sock monkey mojo raring to go. Go wild and get silly!

Acquire all of your sock monkey essentials based on your notes from the Sock Monkey Pal Checklist. Set up a safe cutting and sewing area with your final sock monkey design worksheet in view and materials and supplies close at hand. Be sure to have the technique pages of *basic* and *distinctive* features marked for fast reference while you sew. If you are supervising someone or making a sock monkey jointly with someone, review the 12 Easy Steps on pages 136 to 141 in advance to identify cutting and sewing roles other little or big fingers can assume. Then get yourself comfy, and get ready to rock, sock, cut, and sew!

Should you prewash your socks? If you buy socks in their original package, it is not necessary to prewash them, unless you have allergies or other health concerns. The socks will stay stiffer while you work with them. Only clean your monkey after too many hugs, tugs, or a malady makes a monkey wash necessary. If you decide to prewash, read your sock package for washing instructions or the red-heel sock wash instructions on page 160 if you purchased socks manufactured by NKC or FRM.

SEWING IN GENERAL

Standard-size Sock Monkey

A basic, standard-size sock monkey created from adult-size socks can usually be sewn completely by hand or with the aid of a sewing machine by someone who has minimum to moderate sewing experience. If you use a sewing machine, a monkey can normally be completed within three hours. Creating a monkey with distinctive details typically takes longer.

Use an all-purpose cream-colored thread and a sharp, general-purpose needle to hand-sew monkey parts, seams, and various features. Double thread the needle, pulling one strand of thread through the needle until the thread before and after the needle eye are of the same workable length, then tie the ends together in a knot.

When using embroidery thread to sew on monkey features, separate the desired number of strands from a cut length, thread your needle, and knot only one end.

Parts of a standard-size sock monkey are typically sewn with ¼- to ⅜-inch (6mm to 1 cm) seams. No trimming of excess seams is necessary, except for ear seams, as excess seam material may influence how ears look. Match the alignment of different colors, such as the cream and brown colors of brown heather socks, so the cream and brown colors align on both sides of the seam to be sewn. Sew all seams with small running stitches or backstitches (five to seven stitches per inch [2.5 cm]). Fold raw edges of monkey parts to the inside after they are stuffed, and use small whipstitches to close the ends of all parts before sewing them onto your monkey. If there are monkey parts you choose not to stuff, the raw edges should still be folded to the inside and whipstitched closed. Use small whipstitches to sew all sock parts onto your sock monkey, pushing knots below the surface of the sock to hide them. If your sock monkey is meant to be well loved, then double stitch all seams, sock part closures,

If you want a buddy for life, make sure you give your monkey a body for life. If you are hand-sewing your monkey, sew all seams with small running stitches or backstitches. All monkey parts should be sewn closed and sewn onto your monkey with small whipstitches. Doubling the stitches may double the life of your monkey.

and sock monkey parts for added strength. Double coverage will double your effort, but will help preserve your sock monkey through years of tough love!

If you opt to use a sewing machine to sew the long seams of your monkey, the following information may be helpful:

- Use a universal sewing machine needle size 90/14 or a ballpoint 90/14 if the universal sewing machine needle slips stitches on a practice piece of similar sock scrap.

- Set your stitch length to 3 or 3.5.

- Use an all-purpose cream-colored thread on the spool and in the bobbin.

- Test your machine sewing tension on similar fabric to accommodate proper stitching of a medium-weight sock seam. Tension is normally set from 4 to 4.5, but all machines are different, so your machine's tension setting should be adjusted accordingly. A machine needle is usually changed every ten to twelve hours of use unless the needle is damaged while sewing. Sew with a fresh needle in your machine, if possible.

- Double stitch all seams sewn by machine if your monkey is to be well-loved. Simply run a second line of machine stitches next to the first line of stitches for stability.

Keep a camera handy if you like to take photographs. Snapshots of your cute and collectible monkey in the making will be priceless to you and yours, especially if other little or big hands are helping you make a monkey friend.

Use a length of thick thread, such as embroidery thread (six-ply strands) and an embroidery needle with a large eye to hand-sew button eyes onto your monkey. If you want to add an upswing smile, smile line, eyelashes, eyebrows, eyes, or other features made from embroidery thread, cut workable lengths of the six-ply embroidery strands, and separate the six-ply strands into two sets of three strands by pulling three strands (at one time) away from the six-ply strands. Some features, such as embroidered eyes created with satin stitches, look great with all six-ply strands used, and other features look best with only two or three strands. Experiment with what thickness works for you and your monkey!

Sit in a swivel chair while you sew, if you have one, to enable you to easily turn away from your work surface when you stuff sock monkey parts. This way, you will have room to hold the parts over your lap and rest them on your thighs while you stuff the parts, using your thighs as support.

Remove loose sock nubs and lint from the work area with a spray can of lint remover, small brush, or vacuum.

Use this stitch to hand sew monkey part seams as well as basic and distinctive features such as smile lines and eyebrows. Typically, five to seven backstitches are sewn per inch (2.5 cm).

HAND-SEWN STITCHES
Backstitch
SEAMS

1. Thread your needle with a length of all-purpose thread and knot the thread ends together. Place the right sides of the sock fabric together and align the edges. Hold the seam to be sewn in front of you horizontally.

2. Insert the needle tip up from the underside of the fabric and out through the surface of the fabric on the seam line (approximately ¼ to ³⁄₈ inch [6mm to 1 cm] from the fabric edge).

3. Insert the needle tip down through the surface of the fabric and out a small space away to make one stitch, pulling the thread tight, but not puckering the fabric.

4. Insert the needle tip up from the underside of the fabric and out through the surface of the fabric the same distance away as the length of the first stitch.

5. Insert the needle tip down through the surface of the fabric and out in front of the previous stitch, as close to the stitch as possible, but without touching the threads of the previous stitch. (This backward motion is what defines the backstitch.)

6. Insert the needle tip from the underside of the fabric up and out through the surface of the fabric at a distance to create a stitch the length of the first stitch, but going forward.

7. Repeat steps 5 and 6 until the seam line has been completely sewn, using small stitches of equal length.

8. Knot your thread and cut.

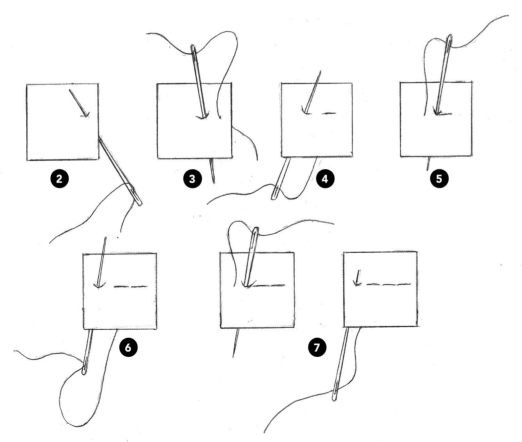

Features embroidered with backstitches are sewn either starting from the surface of the sock fabric when the monkey part has been stuffed or from the underside of the sock fabric before the monkey part has been stuffed. When starting on the surface of the sock fabric, be sure to push your knots under the surface of the sock to hide them, if desired. (When starting and ending stitches on the underside of the sock fabric, this step is not necessary.)

Backstitch

FEATURES ON STUFFED MONKEY PARTS

Use this technique to embroider features such as outlines of tattoos, teeth, and fangs onto stuffed monkey parts.

1. Thread your large-eyed needle with a length of embroidery thread and knot only one end.

2. Insert the needle tip down through the surface of the fabric and up and out a small distance away from the knot to make one stitch, pulling the thread tight, but not puckering the fabric.

3. Insert the needle tip down through the surface of the fabric in front of the knot, but not touching the threads of the knot (this backward motion is what defines the backstitch), and up and out a distance from the knot to equal another stitch.

4. Insert the needle tip down through the surface of the fabric in front of the previous stitch, as close to the stitch as possible without touching the threads of the previous stitch.

5. Repeat steps 3 and 4 until the feature has been completely sewn, using small stitches of equal length.

6. Knot your thread and cut.

7. Push the knots below the sock surface with the blunt end of your needle to hide the knots.

NOTE: *To embroider features such as eyebrows, nose outlines, and smile lines on unstuffed monkey parts, primarily follow the steps on pages 128 and 129.*

French Knots

FEATURES ON UNSTUFFED MONKEY PARTS

1. Thread your milliner or other large-eyed needle with a length of embroidery thread and knot one end.

2. Insert the needle tip up through the material from the underside of the fabric and through the top.

3. Grasp the working thread in your non-needle hand a few inches above the fabric surface. Holding the needle parallel and close to the fabric surface, wrap the thread snugly twice around the needle, wrapping from the eye end toward the tip, and abutt the wraps but do not overlap them. (If you want a larger French knot, wrap the thread three times.)

4. Insert the needle tip down through the fabric very close to (almost on top of) where the thread first came through the surface. Gently pull the working thread so the wraps pull snugly against the fabric.

5. Continue to hold the thread tight in your non-needle hand, as your needle hand pushes the needle all the way through and out the underside of the fabric. (In this way, the thread wraps around the needle stay tightly together and do not misshape as you create a French knot.)

6. Tie off and knot your thread on the underside of the material and cut your thread unless you want to make more than one French knot nearby the French knot you just made. If so, repeat the process beginning with step 2.

Use this stitch to sew distinctive features such as beauty marks, or tiny noses, and ailments such as hives unto unstuffed parts.

Practice this technique several times until you get the hang of it. Once you do, your monkey will be ready for your handiwork—bumps, lumps, and all!

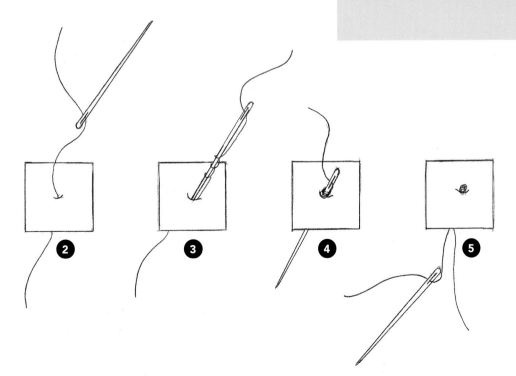

2   3   4   5

Gather Stitch

FEATURES ON STUFFED MONKEY PARTS

1. Thread your needle with a length of all-purpose thread and knot the ends together.

2. Insert your needle tip in and out of the fabric, repeating stitches of equal lengths in the area you want to gather.

3. Pull the thread tight to create gathers until you see the gathered effect you desire. The tighter you pull, the tighter the gather.

4. Knot your thread and cut.

5. Push the knots below the sock surface with the blunt end of your needle to hide the knots.

Use this stitch in a circle to sew an "innie" belly button.

Think of "gathers" as tiny folds of fabric.

GATHER STITCH

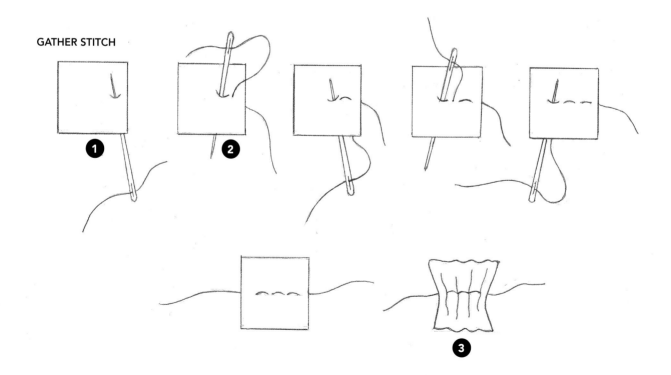

SATIN STITCH

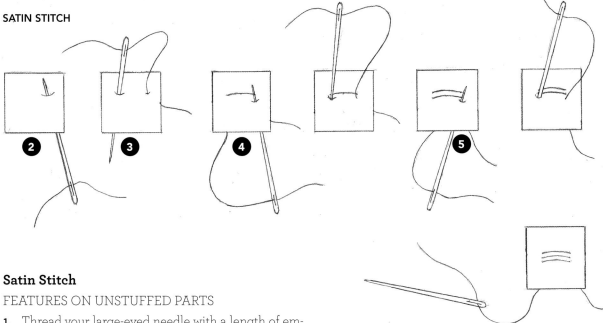

Satin Stitch

FEATURES ON UNSTUFFED PARTS

1. Thread your large-eyed needle with a length of embroidery thread and knot one end.

2. Insert the needle tip up from the underside of the fabric and out through the surface.

3. Sew a single stitch the length of the area you want to cover without puckering the material as you pull the stitch tight.

4. Sew a parallel abutting stitch next to the first stitch as close as possible without placing it on top of the previous stitch.

5. Repeat sewing parallel stitches until you create a solid field of stitches in the desired size with no gaps in between.

6. Knot your thread on the underside of the material and cut.

NOTE: *To embroider features such as teeth or fangs onto the surface of a stuffed part, be sure to push your knots under the surface to hide them, if desired.*

Use this stitch to sew basic and distinctive features such as eyes, noses, and various tattoos and appliqué designs onto unstuffed monkey parts.

If you want the satin-stitched feature to have depth, repeat the steps over the same area one more time.

Running Stitch

SEAMS

1. Thread your needle with a length of all-purpose thread and knot the ends together. Place the right sides of the sock fabric together and align the edges. Hold the seam to be sewn in front of you horizontally.

2. Insert the needle tip up from the underside of the fabric up and out through the surface of the fabric on the seam line (¼ to ⅜ inch [6mm to 1 cm] from the fabric edge).

3. Insert the needle tip down through the surface of the fabric and out a small space away to make one stitch, pulling the thread tight, but not puckering the fabric.

4. Insert the needle tip up from the underside of the fabric and out through the surface of the fabric a shorter distance away than the length of the first stitch.

5. Insert the needle tip down through the surface of the fabric and out to create a stitch the length of the first stitch.

6. Repeat steps 4 and 5 until the seam line has been completely sewn, using small stitches of equal length.

7. Knot the thread and cut.

RUNNING STITCH

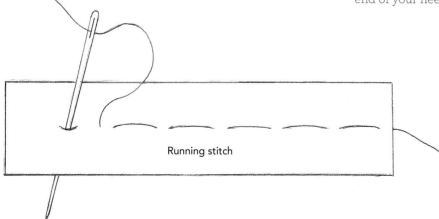

Running stitch

Use this stitch to hand sew monkey part seams as well as basic and distinctive features such as smiles, eyebrows, and trim work made with dashes of thread onto stuffed monkey parts. A typical pace is five to seven running stitches per inch (2.5 cm).

FEATURES ON STUFFED MONKEY PARTS

1. Thread your needle with a length of embroidery thread and knot one end.

2. Insert the needle tip down through the surface of the fabric and up and out a small space away from the knot.

3. Insert the needle tip down through the surface of the fabric a small length away to make one stitch, and up and out a length smaller than the stitch, pulling the thread tight, but not puckering the fabric.

4. Repeat step 3 until the feature has been sewn, using stitches of the same length.

5. Knot your thread and cut.

6. Push the knots below the sock surface with the blunt end of your needle to hide them, if desired.

Whipstitch

1. Thread your needle with a length of all-purpose thread and knot the ends together.

2. Turn the raw fabric edges of the sock monkey parts under ¼ to ⅜ inch (6 to 1 cm) with your fingertips. Pinch the turned edges of the fabric flat against each other with the fingers of one hand.

3. Insert the needle through the turned edges of both pieces of fabric, then bring the needle up, over, and around to the other side of the fabric, and then back through the fabric a short distance away from where you entered the fabric on the other side, pulling the thread tight, but not puckering the fabric.

4. Repeat step 3 until the lengths of fabric are joined together, spacing and sewing the stitches in equal lengths with each stitch typically sewn at a slight diagonal from the other.

5. Knot your thread and cut.

6. Push the knots below the sock surface with the blunt end of your needle to hide them, if desired.

Use this stitch to sew monkey parts closed, to sew parts onto your monkey, and to sew on features such as a moustache, a beard, hair, eyebrows, tattoo patches, and sock caps. Typically, five to seven whipstitches are sewn per inch (2.5 cm).

WHIPSTITCH

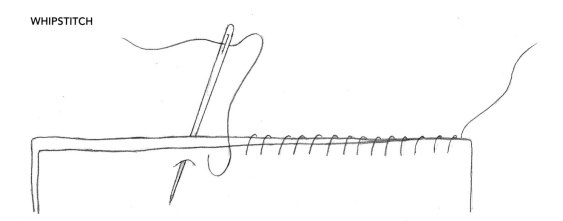

SEWING SPECIFICS: GETTING DOWN TO THE NUBS IN 12 EASY STEPS

Various sock monkey sewing instructions exist in the marketplace, with different patterns on how to cut sock monkey parts from socks. Some instructions require three socks. The sock monkey sewing pattern that follows requires two socks.

Words of encouragement: Keep in mind there is no such thing as an ugly monkey—maybe a *spooktacular* monkey, but not an ugly one! Your creation will be special, unique, and a labor of love. So, whether you create a hero, villain, geeky dude, princess, rock star, or sassy diva, enjoy the sewing process.

You will not be able to start off on the wrong foot! Each sock in a pair is similar in shape and size, so pick one and begin. Use the image you designed of your ideal sock monkey as inspiration. Follow these 12 Easy Steps and your monkey will no longer be imagined, but afoot!

Red-heel socks are quite forgiving; if certain attributes you have sewn or glued onto your monkey do not meet your expectations, stop. Carefully remove the stitch work, quickly remove the glued items before they adhere, wipe away any residue, and resew. Rip out a seam or feature to change characteristics to more *sockitizing* ones even if your creation is in midstream.

12 EASY STEPS

1. Embroider facial embellishments such as eyes, eyelashes, and eyebrows onto the toe area of the first sock. If beauty marks are desired beyond the placement of them in step 7, page 138, add them now. Facial embellishments to be glued, painted, or applied with marker are applied in step 4, after the sock is stuffed. Refer to Diagram 1.

2. Turn the sock inside out, and lay the sock flat with the red-heel side facing up. Insert the needle about ½ inch (1.3 cm) to the right of the center of the sock and about 2 inches (5 cm) below the cream-colored area of the red heel. Sew a seam with running stitches or backstitches toward the end of the white cuff. About ½ inch (1.3 cm) before the end of the cuff, curve the seam outward to form the bottom of the foot and sew to the edge of the sock. Repeat the above about ½ inch (1.3 cm) to the left of the center of the sock and about 2 inches (5 cm) below the cream-colored area of the red heel. Both legs are now sewn but not cut apart. (If your monkey is to have fatter, skinnier, or shapelier legs beyond what sculpting with stuffing will do, adjust where you sew the two leg seams either farther apart or closer together and sew the seams straight or with curves. If your monkey is to have shorter legs, form the bottom of the foot earlier, before you approach the end of the cream-colored cuff.) Refer to Diagram 2.

3. Cut the length of material between the two long leg seams apart, beginning at the end of the cuff, and cut toward the crotch area of your monkey. Cut the length ¼ to ½ inch (6 to 13 mm) longer than the leg seams so the sock can later be turned right side out more easily. Refer to Diagram 3.

1

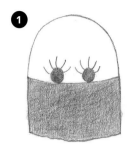   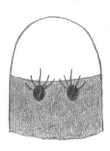 

inside out   inside out   right side out

 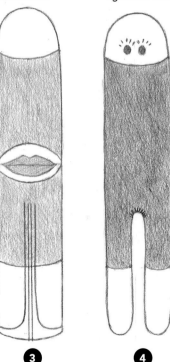

Hand-sewn stitch work is typically five to seven stitches per inch (2.5 cm).

Caution: The sock monkey is not recommended for children under the age of four years old. Accessories such as buttons, pom-poms, and beadwork may cause choking or suffocation. Never give a monkey with small parts to a child or a pet.

②   **③**   **④**

4. Carefully pull the sock right side out through the small open space between the legs, and stuff the entire main body and legs to the desired firmness. (If you plan to paint facial embellishments onto your monkey later, be sure to stuff the body firm to minimize paint cracking due to unwanted shifting of stuffing.) Whipstitch the crotch area closed and reinforce this seam with another set of whipstitches overlapping the first set of whipstitches. Add facial embellishments such as eyelashes, eyes, eyebrows, and beauty marks to be glued, painted, or applied with marker at this time and let dry. Place the main body aside for the moment. Refer to Diagram 4.

(continued)

5. Cut the cap, red-heel mouth piece, tail, arms, and ear parts from the second sock, with the sock right side out. (Adjust the width of the tail part before you cut if you want extra fabric for bigger ear and arm parts.) Cut the arm and ear parts again along the fold of material to provide proportionate pieces for two arms and two ears. Place the cap and red-heel mouth piece aside. Refer to Diagram 5.

6. Place the arms, tail, and ear parts wrong sides together. Sew the arms, tail, and ear seams with running stitches or backstitches. Leave monkey part fabric openings per Diagram 6 to enable you to later stuff these parts. (If you want shorter arms or tail, end arm or tail seams earlier within the cream-colored area of the sock. Or, before you sew these seams, cut the brown-colored ends of each part shorter. If you want your monkey to have fatter, skinnier, or shapelier arms or tail beyond what sculpting with stuffing will do later, adjust where you sew the seams of these parts—either wider apart or closer together—and sew the seams straight or with curves. Trim off the excess seam of each ear to within ¼ inch [6 mm].) Turn all parts right side out. Stuff all parts to the desired firmness. Fold the raw edges of the fabric inside the part about ¼ to ³/₈ inch (6mm to 1 cm) at the end of each part. Sew the ends of all parts closed with small whipstitches to secure the stuffing within and to make parts easier to sew onto the main body of your monkey later. Set the parts aside. Refer to Diagram 6.

7. Pick up the red-heel mouth piece you set aside in step 5. Add facial embellishments, such as a nose, smile lines, and beauty marks to be sewn. Then lightly stuff the red-heel mouth piece, and center it onto the main body under the eyes created in step 1 or step 4. Fold the brown edge of the mouth piece under so only the cream and red-colored areas of the red heel show, and then sew the mouth piece by hand with small whipstitches to the main body. Before the mouth piece is completely sewn onto your monkey, add more stuffing until the desired firmness is achieved. After the mouth piece is sewn onto the monkey, add facial embellishments to the mouthpiece, such as an upswing smile, and features such as a nose, smile lines, beauty marks, and teeth/fangs to be glued, painted, or applied with marker. Allow them to dry. Refer to Diagram 7.

(continued)

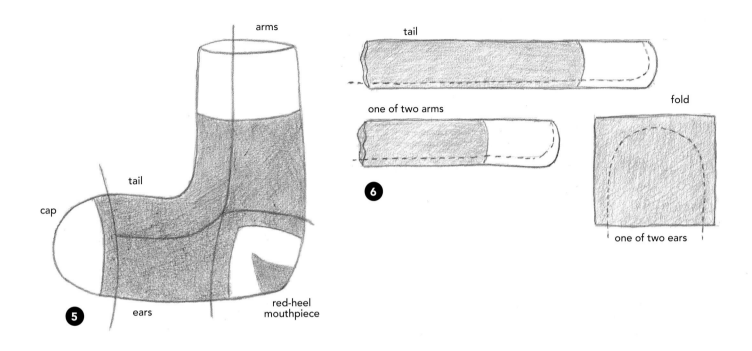

arms

tail

tail

cap

one of two arms

fold

ears

red-heel
mouthpiece

5

6

one of two ears

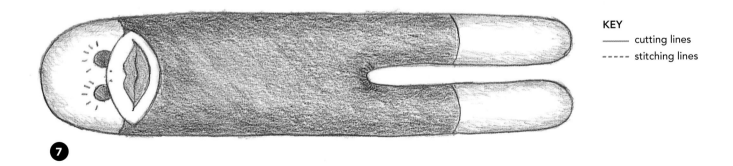

7

KEY

——— cutting lines

- - - - stitching lines

8. Sew the arms, tail, and ears you prepared in step 6 onto the main body at their end seams using small whipstitches. Sew the arms and tail onto your monkey with the long seam of each part on the underside, hidden from view. Refer to Diagram 8.

9. Pick up the sock cap set aside in step 5. Roll up the colored portion of the cap to look like a hat brim. Add cap embellishments at this time, if desired. Add hair to the head of your cute and collectible sock monkey if desired. Place the cap on your monkey's head with the toe seams of the cream-colored area to the right and left sides of the head. Sew the cap to the monkey's head with small whipstitches. Refer to Diagram 9.

10. Apply basic features best applied after the monkey is entirely sewn, such as a neckline tie and pom-poms.

11. Apply distinctive features best applied after the monkey is sewn, such as a belly button, ear hair, eye shadow, teeth, tongue, and rosy cheeks. Sculpt your monkey. Shape your monkey's limbs by hand to form curves and muscles, or cinch shapes if you did not sew a shape into the individual part pieces where an enhanced shape is desired. Sculpt fingers and toes, wrists and ankles. Add other characteristics, such as colorful fingernails and booties, and if desired, apply the initials of your new monkey or your own as the monkey's maker.

12. Clean up, dress, and accessorize your monkey. Remove loose sock nubs, threads, and lint. Most times a flick of the needle can remove brown nubs from showing through the cream-colored sock weave and vice versa. Push the ends of protruding thread below the surface of the sock with a blunt instrument rather than snip the thread off. Remove loose fibers from the surface of your monkey with a lint roller brush.

Before you sew any parts onto your monkey, double-check that each part is placed exactly where you want it on your monkey-to-be!

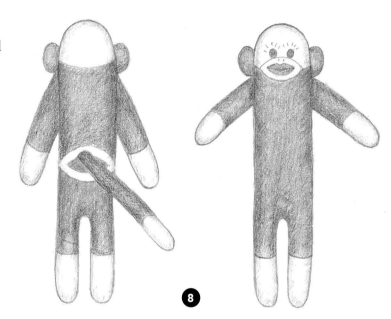

8

TAKE ACCLAIM!

Congratulations! You have completed your cute and collectible sock monkey friend! Can you hear the horns blow or the tumultuous applause? No? Well, perhaps you do not hear fanfare, but you probably feel an inner contentment in your *sole*. In recognition of remarkable artistic achievement, you should take credit for your accomplishment and send your sock monkey friend off into the world with credentials.

In our brand-name society, put your name, with the date your sock monkey was completed, on a tag around your monkey's leg, or embroider, paint, or mark your initials to flatter your monkey's red bum or other designated spot. Heartwarming labels that read "Created with Love" or other sayings can be purchased in most craft and fabric stores or custom-made by label makers. Do whatever works best to rejoice in your accomplishment.

9

Dressing Your Monkey—Sock Monkey Style!

Stitch and Sew Clothes for the *Sole*

While sock monkey villains, heroes, dandies, and dudes look swell in their bare socks, and sock monkey prima donnas, dancers, princesses, and divas look great with all their nubs showing, sock monkeys get a big persona boost when crafters let their fashion designer instincts take hold and deck their monkeys out in colorful duds or dresses.

Sock monkey heroes with magical capes, princesses with glittering tiaras, cowboys in fringed chaps, and debs in sweet dresses all become more endearing and more realistic in character when done up sock monkey style!

To dress your monkey marvel in style, throw out society's preconceived ideas about fashion and style. It's all about self-expression. It's about dressing your new friend to fit today's carefree lifestyle—fast and easy—in trendy and stylish staples! Forget about those perfect stitches, seams, or hems. Baggy, oversized, or way too tight and scanty outfits will look great on your sock monkey friend and will catch the monkey fashion aficionados two-stepping to quick-fix fashionable threads!

CAUTION: Small parts could cause a choking hazard for children under the age of four or pets. Do not give a sock monkey with small parts to a young child or a pet.

The scoop about clothes sock-monkey style is that there are no boundaries. Let your creativity flow and express the fashion designer in you. If you think it, design it! Instant outfits can be made from sparkling hair cozies, headbands, and ribbon. Holiday ribbon and garland can double as tube tops and miniskirts—or even a head of hair! Go tropical and create cool sarongs or stylish togas—fold and tie bandanas, beautiful hankies, scarves, or snips of material for a look to be admired!

Create monkey clothes in a smoke- and pet-free environment, especially if you create clothes for a monkey to be gifted.

Enter this glamorous world where outfits constructed from swatches of fabric, fringe, ribbons, strands, and bands are boss! Think freestyle—think out of the ordinary. Think easy, simple outfits to cut, tie, and go. Think a hook and loop fastener here, a dab of glue there, a fanciful button sewn here, or maybe a tuck and a few quick stitches there—all done with flair. Then add glitzy ornamentation for trim or accessories and wow the world with your one-of-a-kind ensemble fashioned sock monkey style!

Whether your budget is big or small, you can create a wardrobe to befit the character of your new cute and collectible monkey. Fun and funky creative clothing and accessory solutions are plentiful, and quick-fix fashion ideas and projects await crafters' designing hands. Crafters or caregivers with little time can purchase ready-to-wear clothes. If you have new threads in mind, but don't have the time, do not fret! Your sock monkey pal does not need a whole wardrobe overnight. Let the wardrobe evolve naturally or let your monkey go au naturale!

NO-PATTERN, QUICK-FIX FASHIONS

A menagerie of no-pattern, quick-fix fashions for your magnificent monkey awaits your magical imagination! Choose from a smorgasbord of no-pattern, quick-fix ideas to create cute and funky clothes within minutes that will knock your socks off. Will your monkey be a quick-change artist and have a wardrobe of many disguises, or be dressed like someone you know? Whatever persona you choose, your cute and collectible sock monkey attire is sure to reflect the fashion designer in you!

First, go on the trail, like Tex, and track down items from around the house that have accumulated over the years, such as trim, rickrack, fringe, lace, ribbons, and bows. Also collect unwanted but usable items in good, clean condition, such as hair bows, hair bands, ponytail holders, hair scrunchies, bow ties, shoelaces, hankies, and scarves. Don't overlook sentimental items, defunct eyewear, jewelry pieces (toy, real, or otherwise), and other glitzy doodads you might be able to incorporate into your fashions. Check the attic or toy box for old clothes, doll or stuffed animal clothes, and other treasures. If your stash of possibilities is scanty, check with friends and family members to see what sock monkey riches they may have tucked away waiting for you to claim!

This is where more fun begins, as each item you gather might have an essential place in your sock monkey wardrobe now or in the future. So let go of any preconceived ideas about what will make cool sock monkey threads, and hold this thought while you dive into your eclectic pile of items: You have already created your ideal cute and collectible sock monkey from the folds of a pair of socks, so surely assembling an outfit from these gathered items is within your abilities, too. Yes, it is!

If you need a big jump-start for sewing inspiration, hold a fashion design party among friends or family to stitch and sew sock monkey clothes with *sole*. Ask attendees to bring supplies such as fun fabric, handkerchiefs, hair bands, ribbons, buttons, silk flowers, appliqués, beads, trim, shoelaces, and other doodads to add to the wardrobe pile. Each of you could make your own outfits or pass an outfit around for everyone to add to creatively. Exquisite creations are deceptively simple to fashion and will make your sock monkey shine on the runway of life!

There are many ways to quickly and inexpensively dress your sock monkey with style and create a stunning outfit without using a pattern, without leaving home, and without making any purchases at all. For example, Edgar's apparel was created with grade-school glasses from the 1960s and a bow tie from the 1950s that were "relics" of family members.

maybe even as the actual gift if someone heard your *sock-felt* wishes!

Review the showy photographs of sock monkeys throughout chapters 15 and 16, wherein monkeys are dressed in wardrobes created with little to no fuss. Whether you are a big or little crafter, an organization, or an institute, experience how easy it is to get caught up in some sweet Hanky-Panky, Boss-It-Up, Mix-It-Up, and other simple fashions.

Nearly all of these garments tie, slip, or button on and require little to no cutting and sewing. Most pieces could also be glued, stapled, taped, or held together by hook and loop fasteners.

As you sift through the items, focus on making one sock monkey ensemble or more. Keep your sock monkey close by to model various items for size and effect. If you are missing a certain piece to make an outfit complete, you could make a purchase or wait until the essential item, be it a colorful ribbon or bow, miraculously comes through your front door as part of the wrappings of a future gift, or

Tip

If you want to play some hanky-panky, but don't have the hankies, then cut no-fray material into large squares. If you have a to-die-for piece of fabric with raw edges, hide the edges with tape or trim, fringe the edges, or leave them "as is."

Making quick-fix fashions sock monkey style is a breeze! Once the basic garment is constructed, add personal embellishments to create unique, one-of-a-kind garments made especially by you! If you construct plain clothes, go a step further and sew or glue false, colorful striped or polka-dot collars and pockets onto your creations. Trim clothing articles with embellishments such as fringe, lace, appliqués, buttons, tape, or colorful ribbon, or adorn your creations with glitzy gems or beads. Add your own scribbles with fabric paint to jazz up vests, skirts, and cloaks. Start simple and get more elaborate and fanciful as your sock monkey mojo revs up. Or let your monkey be unencumbered and simply show off its trendy threads. The choice is yours!

No patterns and no fuss!

HANKY-PANKY

BOSS-IT-UP

Wired ribbon is great to use on monkeys created for caregivers older than four years of age. Blunt the wire ends by rolling or turning their ends inward, then fold and crimp the ribbon into the desired shape. If wanted, crimp the ends of the ribbon together, like the Boss's patriotic vest, and join the ends. If you are making a sock monkey vest, use wide wired ribbon and simply cut slits for armholes.

MIX-IT-UP

NO-FRAY FABULOUS FABRICS

If you want to use store-bought fabrics for quick-fix items or make sock monkey clothes from your own patterns, like wrestlers "Smiley" Socks Grogan and "Biter" Blacky Bart, go to your favorite fabric shop and browse the aisles of material. Ask the store assistant(s) questions about what textiles have no-fray attributes to include in your designs. You will be astounded by the vast selection of felt, polyester fleece, cotton flannel, nylon net, faux fur, leather, and other trendy fabric choices available. View the following Fold and Go and HeartFELT Designs for "no-fray" inspiration.

Fold and Go Designs

HeartFELT Designs

NO-FUSS *SOCKAHOLIC* SHOP STOPS

Sockaholics can easily grow their sweet or swanky sock monkey's wardrobe and accessories as they browse and shop the aisles of favorite stores, surf the Internet, or ask friends or family who sew, crochet, or knit to create something special. When your feet or fingers are doing the walking, check out new or like-new doll clothes, preemie baby clothes, teddy bear clothes, and other similarly sized stuffed animal clothes.

Browse the dog aisles for doggie jackets and doggie shoes to fit extra-small dogs—you will be surprised at how doggie wear designs, like Bony's, fit sock monkeys created from adult-size socks! Even "goose" clothes, like Goldie's will work! Mix and match new and like-new apparel to create fashion-savvy sock monkey ensembles. And if you have exhausted your search for special sock monkey outfits to fit your new friend, ask a seamstress to custom-make a monkey suit to your specification.

Potential stops:

- Your own household treasures!
- Festivals, bazaars, flea markets, estate sales, and garage sales
- Community thrift stores
- Internet websites
- Stuffed bear specialty shops
- Pet shops
- Department stores and shops that carry ready-made dog jackets, goose wear, preemie baby clothes, doll clothes, bear clothes, and accessories
- Party celebration shops for accessories

More quick ideas? Cut off the toe area of a tube sock or the fingers of gloves for an instant dress.

Take your sock monkey friend with you to the store to be "size-wise." You'll be the center of attention when your monkey sits in the baby seat of your cart!

Don't Forget to Colorize and Accessorize!

Think about the whole persona of your monkey. Get *sockitude* and give your monkey attitude! As you pull together your sock monkey's wardrobe, go bananas with color and accessories. Get gaudy! Be extravagant! Fabrics and ribbons of brilliant solids, screaming squares, bright neon stripes, and perky polka dots add to the playfulness and humor of what sock monkeys are all about.

Make your sock monkey outfits pop with glitter and glitz! Ornate buttons, glitzy trim, fringe, rickrack, beads, appliqués, and adhesive or sew-on gems will add sparkle to your "aww-some" creations. False pockets, false collars, mock belts, and other clothing features will rid you of pre-runway jitters because they can hide myriad sewing or size imperfections. From the top of your sock monkey's head to the bottom of your monkey's feet and tippy tail, add colorful finishes such as hair ribbons, showy bow ties, watches, garters, socks, and shoes to put the razzle in your sock monkey's dazzle! Even simple hats, scarves, and mitten ensembles are snazzy winners.

A fun time to acquire props is after each holiday. Check out the holiday clearance aisles after Valentine's Day, St. Patrick's Day, Easter, Fourth of July, Halloween, Thanksgiving, and Christmas. You will be surprised by what you find!

If your cute and collectible monkey is a special gift, personalize it. Add beaded earrings, a necklace, and wrist or ankle bracelets. For something very special, add jewelry in the letters of the intended caregiver's name.

Monogram your monkey's cap or vest with your monkey's moniker or the recipient's name or initials. Create clothing in the caregiver's favorite colors or favorite team colors. If you are making the monkey for someone who wears glasses, give your monkey four eyes, too!

And don't forget about props! Tune in to your monkey's persona—give your darling diva her glasses and purse, a chic uptown girl her designer bag, and a rock star his guitar. When done, turn on the runway lights and release your dressed creation for others to enjoy!

Nip and Tuck

Sentimental crafters who have vintage hankerchiefs from granddaddy, great granny's jewelry, or darling baby outfits and shoes tucked away in an old trunk can dress and accessorize their sock monkeys with a bit of treasured family nostalgia. Quick nips and tucks to adjust items to sock monkey size will make them great heirloom keepsakes.

Check out more photographs in Glitter Glamour and Snazzy Simple on pages 156 and 157 to see how easy it is to colorize and accessorize!

Garments and accessories fashioned from your family's or ancestors' clothing make great conversation pieces, especially when the model is your cute and collectible *sole* mate!

Glitter Glamour

Snazzy Simple

About the Author

Known as the Sock Monkey Lady®, Dee Lindner is an author, photographer, and artist whose medium is handmade red-heel sock monkeys. She has over twenty-five years of successful experience in the marketplace and a portfolio of hundreds of sock monkey images of her collection and creations. Published books, journals, boxed cards, note cards, greeting cards, book marks, valentine packs, checks, and more have been produced using her art. Her sock monkey-themed, action-oriented photography has been licensed by major publishers, including Andrews McMeel Publishing; Peter Pauper Press; Peaceable Kingdom; Galison; and Bradford Check Exchange, LTD. Also, Barnes & Noble has carried her images as holiday cards.

ACKNOWLEDGMENTS

A hearty thanks to sock monkey enthusiasts and crafters everywhere, for without their collective creative imagination, energy, exuberance, and stories, our socks would still be in our drawers. And finally, thank you to my clients and to the many crafty people whose *sockpendous* sock monkeys are in my collection.

KNOCK-KNOCK JOKE

Knock-knock.
Who's there?

Dewey.
Dewey who?

When do we monkey around?
Now is the time to sock, rock, cut, and sew!

The end!
Happy Crafting!

Appendix

DETAILED LOOK AT SOCK DIFFERENCES

NELSON KNITTING COMPANY

- Upswing to edges of red color in the red-heel area
- Larger cream-colored area surrounding red-heel area
- Larger cream-colored area in toe area
- Inside seam differences
- Adult-size red-heel sock colors: blue, gray, red/green, green/red, white, variegated blue, and brown heather
- Miniature red-heel sock colors: blue and brown heather.
- Packaging: Many of NKC's red-heel socks were sold singly, without packaging, with only a price tagged on each pair by retail outlets. Single pairs, two pairs, three pairs, and even six pairs of red-heel socks were also packaged in poly bags or bands with pamphlet instructions on how to sew a sock monkey and a sock elephant.
- Content: 100% cotton with references, at times, of 2% nylon in the toes.
- Care: Machine wash warm, tumble dry.

FOX RIVER MILLS, INC.

- Elongated oval for red color in the red-heel area
- Smaller cream-colored area surrounding red-heel area
- Smaller cream-colored area in toe area
- Inside seam differences
- Adult-size red-heel sock colors: blue, pink, red, yellow, green, and brown heather
- Child-size small red-heel sock colors: brown mini
- Early packaging: Packaged two pairs in a poly bag with pamphlet instructions on how to sew a sock monkey and a sock elephant. In addition, the socks were also sold in large unpackaged quantities.

  Content: 97% cotton, 2% acrylic, 1% nylon, except 2% Lycra spandex added to tops.

  Care: Machine wash warm, no bleach, tumble dry, no heat.

  Later packaging: Packaged in cardboard top riders with instructions on how to sew a sock monkey printed on the inside of the cardboard riders. In addition, the socks are also sold in large unpackaged quantities.

  Content: 87% cotton, 7% polyester, 3% nylon, 2% acrylic, 1% spandex.

  Care: Machine wash warm, inside out. Tumble dry on low. Do not bleach, iron, or dry clean.

FACIAL FEATURE DESIGNS

EYES

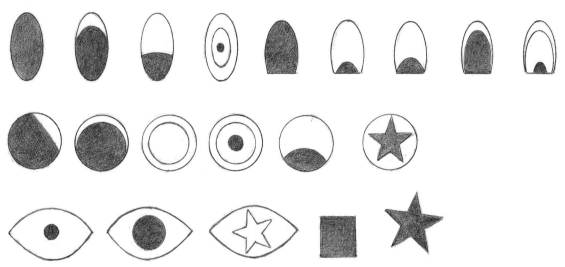

Adjust sizes as desired

EYELASHES

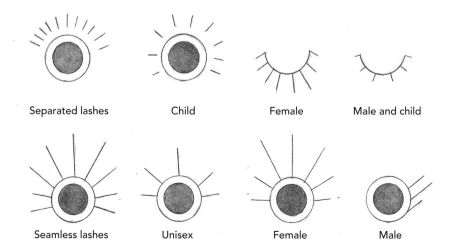

Separated lashes   Child   Female   Male and child

Seamless lashes   Unisex   Female   Male

SMILES

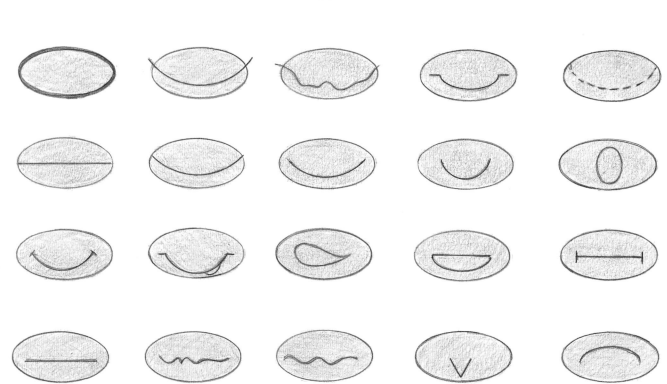

NOSES

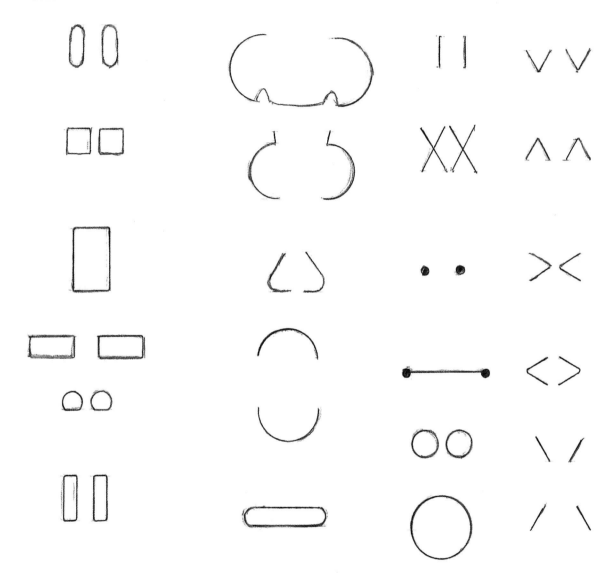

EYEBROWS

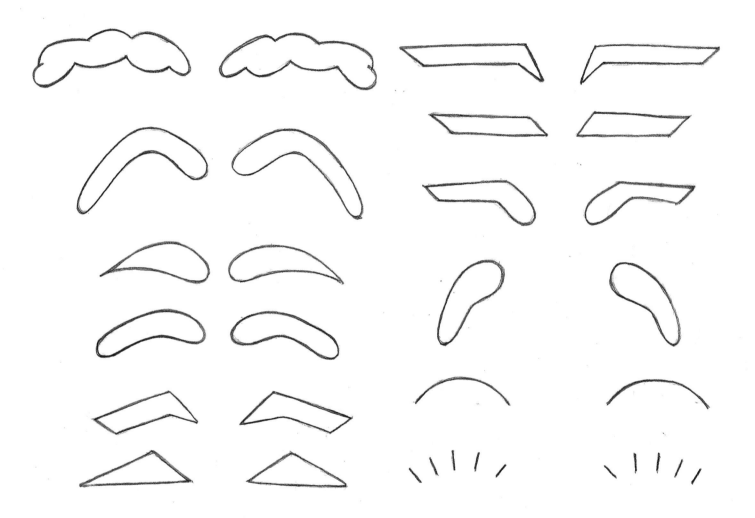

MOUSTACHES

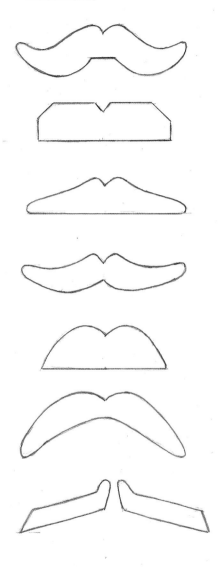

OTHER DESIGNS

TATTOOS

HAT BRIM

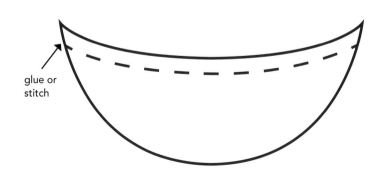

glue or
stitch

Index

Also Available:

The Ultimate Sock Puppet Book
978-1-58923-793-3

Amigurumi Knits
978-1-58923-435-2

Bead Bugs
978-1-58923-732-2

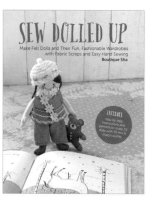

Sew Dolled Up
978-1-58923-872-5

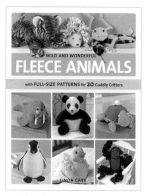

Wild and Wonderful Fleece Animals
978-1-58923-578-6

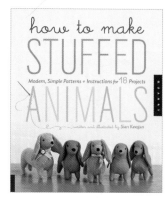

How to Make Stuffed Animals
978-1-59253-799-0

Wool Pets
978-1-58923-525-0

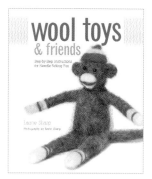

Wool Toys and Friends
978-1-58923-506-9

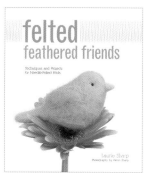

Felted Feathered Friends
978-1-58923-694-3